John A. Weaver

Popular Culture
PRIMER

PETER LANG
New York • Washington, D.C./Baltimore • Bern
Frankfurt am Main • Berlin • Brussels • Vienna • Oxford

Library of Congress Cataloging-in-Publication Data

Weaver, John A.
Popular culture primer / John A. Weaver.
p. cm.
Includes bibliographical references.
1. Popular culture. 2. Culture—Study and teaching. I. Title.
HM621.W38 2005   306—dc22   2004016764
ISBN 0-8204-7114-3 (paperback)
ISBN 0-8204-7642-0 (hardcover)

Bibliographic information published by **Die Deutsche Bibliothek**.
Die Deutsche Bibliothek lists this publication in the "Deutsche
Nationalbibliografie"; detailed bibliographic data is available
on the Internet at http://dnb.ddb.de/.

Cover design by Lisa Barfield

The paper in this book meets the guidelines for permanence and durability
of the Committee on Production Guidelines for Book Longevity
of the Council of Library Resources.

Printed in the United States of America

Popular Culture
PRIMER

PETER LANG
New York • Washington, D.C./Baltimore • Bern
Frankfurt am Main • Berlin • Brussels • Vienna • Oxford

Table of Contents

From Culture and Images to Popular Culture Images

Culture

"a particular way of life which expresses certain meanings and values not only in art and learning, but also in institutions and ordinary behaviour" (Williams, *The Long Revolution*, 1961).

Cultural Capital

a term coined by the French sociologist Pierre Bourdieu to describe how people define the meaning of culture to obtain and maintain power in society.

Since the advent of the term "Western Civilization," there has been an attempt to distinguish between the **culture** of those with power and those without it. For those in power, their beliefs, morals, and tastes were sanctioned as the right forms of culture or signified as Culture with a capital "C." This Culture represented a set of social codes in which those people who were Cultured knew the right books to read, the proper ways to interact at social gatherings, the proper forms of dress, the holiest way to worship a god, the correct modes of speech, and the proper culinary tastes. It was these codes, or what Pierre Bourdieu calls **cultural capital**, that marked their possessors as privileged from other people. The people, often referred to condescendingly as "the masses," who did not understand or share these sanctioned values possessed their own social codes, but these codes did not have the same power and therefore the same weight in society to persuade or influence opinions.

Since the twentieth century, this Culture has been challenged. The Culture still exists, but the influence of

aristocratic or traditional tastes on its definition has been limited. Now, popular culture has a much more dramatic influence on how Culture is defined. This introductory chapter will chart the rise of the notion of Culture, discuss its decline, delve into the rise of popular culture as a definer of taste, cover the role that images play in creating meaning, and discuss the term "cultural studies."

Culture: From Plato to Alan Bloom

In *The Republic*, Plato was one of the first Western thinkers to demarcate between proper culture and popular culture. Proper culture for Plato was associated with philosophy. Philosophy was the mode of thinking that assured individuals that they would live a life of truth. It was through philosophy that one would imitate truth rather than partake in the act of mimesis, or the imitation of imitation. Anything that promoted the imitation of truth should be accepted into the ideal city of the Republic and, conversely, anything that was mimetic should be banned. Philosophy taught everyone the right disciplines to study (e.g., calculation, astronomy, geometry, music, and gymnastics). These disciplines would reveal the truth of the universe to everyone and would explain the true calling of each person within the Republic.

Plato's *Republic* is often referred to as a political treatise, but in reality it should be treated as an educational doctrine on how to cultivate the right tastes in the minds of the young. Education should start as early as possible because in early youth the mind is most plastic. It is during this early period that the "right education" or that which imitated the truth, should enter the minds of the young and establish a firm foundation so that these children could recognize the mimetic and reject it as erroneous. To ensure that the young would receive the right education, Plato believed the curriculum should be strictly censored. Myths and heroic tales were accepted only if these tales taught the young to imitate truth. Those myths and tales that spoke of the infallibility of the gods and taught the fear of Hades to the young would be acceptable.

It was also acceptable to teach those tales that reinforced in the minds of the young that the order of the Republic (i.e., guardians rule, soldiers defend, and artisans farm, bake, and build) was not ordered by the philosophers but ordained by the gods.

Those myths and tales that did not promote the imitation of truth were to be banned from the Republic. This meant that the spokespersons of these stories, poets, were also to be banned. Poets, along with painters, were the most dangerous people for Plato. Poets and painters were considered to live far from the truth because they did not imitate the truth but were imitators of imitations. For instance, in Book Three, Plato states that poets should be banned from the city because they do not always speak in their own voices and because they put words in the mouths of gods. When poets speak in other voices, they are deceiving their audiences rather than speaking the truth.

It is Plato's quest to ban poets and painters from the Republic that marks the first attempt to demarcate between Culture and popular culture. In the final book of *The Republic,* Plato justifies his desire to ban poets and painters and thereby raises concerns and opinions that will resonate in debates over popular culture today. First, Plato wishes to ban painting because "the painter . . . will paint for us a shoemaker, a carpenter, and the craftsmen, although he doesn't understand the arts of any one of them . . . [B]y painting a carpenter and displaying him from far off, he would deceive children and foolish human beings into thinking that it is truly a carpenter" (Bloom, 1968, p. 281). According to Plato, people are easily duped into believing what they see. If people see something they will do it. A similar argument is raised today when the media reports that Dylan Klebold and Eric Harris watched the film *Natural Born Killers* before they went on their rampage at Columbine High School in Littleton, Colorado. Although there are roughly 2,400 years separating the writing of *The Republic* and the Columbine massacre, the assumptions are the same: people are not intelligent enough to discern between what is real and what is fantasy.

Just as painters are mimetic, so are poets. For Plato, a poet is a "charming chap . . . but all the same, he will imitate, although he doesn't know in what way each thing is bad or good. But as it seems, whatever looks to be fair to the many who don't know anything—that he will imitate" (Bloom, 1968, p. 285). Like Charlie Chaplin, the Greek poet can persuade anyone, but what is his value in contributing to the good of society? For Plato, the poet offers nothing to elevate society; instead, he will only pander to the lowly tastes and desires of the masses.

Besides playing to the low standards of the masses, the poet is seductive. Plato suggests, "When even the best of us hear Homer or any other of the tragic poets imitating one of the heroes in mourning . . . you know that we enjoy it and that we give ourselves over to following the imitation" (Bloom, 1968, p. 289). The poet seduces us into accepting anything that we hear or see; even the most Cultured of us are entranced by the power of the poet. When Madonna and, earlier, Elvis Presley became popular, critics suggested that they brought out the base emotions of their audiences. The idea behind such criticism is that Culture must be approached with constraint, while popular culture panders to our primitive tastes and desires.

After Plato, the German philosopher Immanuel Kant took up the mantle as the defender of Culture. In his treatise *Conflict of the Faculties*, Kant is often given credit for penning the first statement in defense of academic freedom. However, it is also an open statement that purposely constructs academics as guardians of taste against the masses, who are incapable of discerning between Culture and **kitsch**. Like Plato, Kant viewed natural (mathematics and science) and moral philosophy as the only routes to obtaining Culture. It was implied that Cultured people possessed the ability to properly use their freedom to think rationally. Writing in autocratic Prussia in the late 18th century, Kant wrote his views in a way that granted academics the freedom to express themselves while denying the majority of citizens the same freedom in order to not threaten the authority of the Prussian king. For Kant, freedom and rational thought were beyond average people.

Kitsch

a German word that means cheap or trashy art, but in the United States it has come to signify trendy, accessible, and popular art.

While the Cultured person knew how to exercise his or her freedoms, the average person possessed little or no desire to do so. "The people conceived of their welfare, not primarily as freedom, but as [the realization of] their natural ends," Kant concluded (1979, p. 49), "and so as these three things: being happy after death, having their possessions guaranteed by public laws during their life in society, and finally, looking forward to the physical enjoyment of life itself." People were too base to properly enjoy the life of a Cultured person. Instead, they "want to be led, that is . . . they want to be duped. But they want to be led not only by the scholars of the faculties (whose wisdom is too high for them), but by the businessman of the faculties—clergymen, legal officials, and doctors—who understand a botched job" (Kant, 1978, p. 51). The average person, according to Kant, simply wants to be entertained; to go through life led by anyone who will make him or her laugh. Kant may have been the first person to reveal this disdain for the majority of people, but it is an argument that will continue to be raised by the **Frankfurt School** of critical thought and contemporary critics such as William Bennett, Alan Bloom, and George Will. For these critics, popular culture is interpreted as a sign of moral and Cultural decline.

By the late nineteenth century, many of the arguments Plato and Kant raised against "the masses" and for the Cultured class continued to be developed in Western nations. However, one notable transition occurred during this period. By the 1870s, it was no longer philosophy that would create Culture but literature and the liberal arts tradition. The most ardent supporters of this argument were found in England. In his classic treatise on education and culture, *Culture and Anarchy*, Matthew Arnold embodies the traditional notion of Culture. Often misunderstood as a person who believed that only a few people could ever possess Culture, which meant the mastering of "the best that has been said and thought in our time," Arnold was a superintendent of schools for England in the mid-1800s and traveled to other nations, including France and Germany. He also wrote extensively about schools in

Frankfurt School consisted of a group of sociologists, philosophers, anthropologists, and music scholars who formed one of the major traditions in 20th-century cultural studies.

Europe. Arnold believed that for England to fulfill its potential, English public schools should adopt a curriculum that nurtured perfection in all of its citizens. Perfection was Culture for Arnold, and perfection "consists in becoming something rather than in having something, in an inward condition of the mind and spirit, not in an outward set of circumstances" (Arnold, 1994, p. 33). This inward condition was simultaneously a rejection of the outward materialism that gripped and stymied the minds of most Europeans and a submission to that which embodied sweetness and light: poetry and literature. Yet Arnold did not believe that this goal could be attained. He believed the English placed too much "faith in machinery" and viewed machinery as "if it had a value in and for itself" (Arnold, 1994, p. 34). Because of this vulgar **instrumentalism**, Arnold believed that school reformers would introduce a curriculum that merely swayed students to think and act in the manner that conformed to prevailing ideologies of the times instead of breeding "real" culture in the minds of people. For the curriculum reforms to be true, Arnold believed schools must introduce people to what we would call today a liberal arts education or the "Great Books" approach to education. Arnold's attempts to introduce a more demanding curriculum in English schools eventually failed, but his ideas on the nurturing of the mind and on education as an inward endeavor continue to represent what it means to be a Cultured person in society.

Arnold's successors were not as optimistic when it came to transforming the public school curriculum. Arnold believed that the majority of people, if challenged and motivated, could cultivate their minds to fully understand the "sweetness and light" of literature and poetry, but his successors believed a Cultured education should be limited to the chosen few who demonstrated the desire and ability to understand the mystic beauty of Western canonical treasures. F.R. Leavis, who educated such future British cultural studies founders as Raymond Williams and Richard Hoggart, was one of the leading advocates of this more exclusive approach to education and cultivation.

Instrumentalism

a term used to describe the prevailing idea that an education ought not to necessarily cultivate the mind but prepare a person for a specific vocation.

Like Arnold, Leavis rejected the idea that education should serve instrumental or mechanical purposes. Instead, he advocated what he called the "the essential-university function." This essential function of the university was to "foster [a] collaborative heuristico-creative interplay" between the "educated public" and literature (Leavis, 1982, p.180). From this interpretive interaction would emerge a life worth living. This "life worth living" could be found only in a cultured elite and any university that attempted to function on democratic principles simply could not create a Cultured public.

Another advocate of a Cultured elite was Leo Strauss. For Strauss, "Culture means derivatively and today chiefly the cultivation of the mind, the taking care and improving of the native faculties of the mind in accordance with the nature of the mind." One took care and improved the mind by entering into a figurative conversation with "the greatest minds" of the world through study. "Such men are extremely rare," Strauss wrote. "We are not likely to meet any of them in any classroom." Instead, those who nurtured the mind would converse with these superior thinkers by "studying with the proper care the great books which these greatest of minds have left behind" (Strauss, 1968, p. 3). This conversation was limited to a select few who knew how to listen to the "monologues" of the great minds and who were great "impresarios or lion tamers" of the great books (Strauss, 1968, p. 8). From this ability to listen and interpret would emerge Cultured elites who could lead all democracies. The majority of people possessed neither the ability or desire to listen and interpret nor the natural talents to rule in a democracy. Any form of government that permitted the majority to partake in the decision-making process was not a true democracy and was ruled by the mob. The task of the "uncultured" for Strauss was to accept the edicts and wisdom of those destined to rule.

If, for Strauss, a liberal arts education created a Cultured elite designed to rule, it also acted as "the counterpoison to mass culture, to the corroding effects of mass culture, to its inherent tendency to produce nothing but

specialists without spirit or vision and voluptuaries without heart" (Strauss, 1968, p. 5). Popular culture was created to entertain the masses while the elite ruled. For Strauss, nothing good came from "the noise, the rush, the thoughtlessness" of mass culture. To counteract the constant threat of popular culture, Strauss put his faith in the Cultured few who had the wisdom to keep the tide of anarchy and decline from overtaking contemporary Western democracies.

Strauss' protégé, Alan Bloom, continued his mentor's rant against popular culture. In his book *The Closing of the American Mind* (1988), Bloom chronicles the decline of the elite universities in the United States. To use Strauss' words, Bloom believed that the "natural" elites of the United States stopped listening and interpreting the great minds of the past. Instead, elite students had become relativists, willing to accept any argument presented to them as truth and afraid to offend anyone with whom they disagreed. The torchbearers of the liberal-arts education and Culture had begun to read detective novels, comics, and romances along with the Bible and other great literature. They had stopped listening to classical music and turned to the noise of rock-and-roll. At stake in these tragic shifts of taste, for Bloom, was not only traditional Culture, but also the fundamental belief that a democracy is best when ruled by its natural elite. The Cultured elite of the United States was willfully dumbing itself down. The dominant culture was now popular culture. For Bloom, this change from a liberal-arts tradition of Culture to the adoption of popular culture marked the end of Western dominance in the world. The counterpoison that Strauss saw in the liberal arts was no longer an effective antidote.

The Fall of Culture and the Rise of Popular Culture

Leavis and Strauss were much more optimistic than Bloom about the power of the liberal-arts tradition to protect Cultured society from the corrosive effects of popular culture, even though the decline of Cultured society began during the time that Leavis and Strauss were writing. There are numerous reasons why popular culture became a powerful force in society in the mid-1900s. First, all the major forms of mass communication were developed during this time. By 1950, film, radio, and television were all established elements of American and European culture. Before these forms of entertainment and information dissemination were mass produced, it was easy to demarcate between a Cultured elite and the mass public. In the early 1800s, the mass public was banned from going to museums in England. The belief was that the public could not understand the meaning and importance of museum exhibits. It was not until the mid- to late 1800s that the general public was allowed to visit museums, and even then it was only because of a shift in thinking among the Cultured elite who had come to believe that museums could tame and educate the rough masses. Other forms of entertainment were also limited in their scope. The opera was limited to people who could find the free time to attend a performance. The same was true for live theater. Attending a stage performance often depended on the availability of leisure time and disposable income to pay for the performance. These limitations disappeared with the advent of film, radio, and television. By the 1910s, films were produced and distributed widely enough that anyone could view a single- or double-reel film for a nickel or less. Thus began the creation of a new kind of Cultured elite: vaudeville and traveling actors turned film stars, such as Charlie Chaplin, "Fatty" Arbuckle, Marie Dressler, Max Sennett, Mary Pickford, and the Keystone Cops. By the 1920s, radios were common in households and offered free news and entertainment. By the 1950s, televisions also had become common. With these three modes of communication, people did not have to go to the local opera house to hear Caruso sing or the see the Barrymores perform on Broadway. The artists could be seen on screen, heard on the radio, or watched on television at little or no cost.

A second reason for the decline of Culture was the **Americanization of culture**. Numerous meanings are applied to this term, but here it will be explored in technological terms only. Although the first film was created by

Americanization of Culture

often implies the destruction of local, non-American cultures and the globalization of American culture as the only form of culture.

the Lumaire brothers in France, and radio and television would not be possible without the scientific contributions of Europeans, the scope of these forms of technology were enhanced in America. Edison Park and, later, Hollywood transformed film production into another factory industry. This insured that people throughout the United States and Europe could view the latest Chaplin, Lon Chaney Sr., Mary Pickford, or Douglas Fairbanks picture soon after it was produced. Chaplin, Pickford, and Fairbanks became international stars because of the ability to mass-produce their films and market them to theaters across the globe at the same time. Traditionally, if people wanted to listen to Caruso or see the Barrymores on stage, they would have to wait until they performed in a city nearby, or they would have to travel to New York or London to see them. With film, Chaplin could make *Modern Life* or *The Great Dictator* and simultaneously be in London, New York, Rome, Berlin, and every small town in the world with a movie house. It was this ability to create new stars that undermined the power of opera and stage performers to garner international attention. The same was true with radio and television. Cultured figures became just as common as screen actors. Traditional artists lost their aura as "bigger than life" demigods, while actors who were heard on radio or seen on television became more powerful as the "people's" actors.

Another explanation for the decline of Culture and the rise of popular culture is that the critics of popular culture such as Arnold were correct in their analysis. Arnold rejected an education that was based in instrumentalism, but the reality of the educational systems in Europe and the United States shows that this is exactly what happened. Today, a liberal-arts education can be found, but the dominant reason people get a higher education is to find a job. Liberal-arts courses such as philosophy, romance languages, and history are taken either as basic core courses or as electives and rarely as a foundation for the construction of a Cultured mind. These fields of study have been reduced to instrumental purposes. The importance of philosophy has been reduced to ethics, romance languages to

learning Spanish for business transactions, and history for "critical-thinking skills."

A final explanation is that popular culture could be as Cultured as any of the traditional arts. Initially, when film appeared on the scene it was condemned as inferior to live stage performances, and many stage stars refused to make films. As film became more acceptable and creative people such as Chaplin, Cecil B. DeMille, Alice Gee, Francis Marion, and Lon Chaney Sr. showed what could be created on film, many people changed their minds about it. Similarly, radio, which was regarded originally as a medium to transmit information or broadcast sporting events, was rarely seen as a medium to transmit culture. As people began to experiment with programming, radio producers soon discovered that it was a perfect medium for reading dramas and comedy routines.

Television was different. Early producers such as Gilbert Seldes viewed television as a mode of communication to promote cultural programs. The early period has often been touted as the "golden age of television" for its creative programming and excellent writing. Since this period of early television most critics believe television has been on a steady decline in its creation of taste. One could easily point to "reality" television or talk shows as proof of this decline. Yet even with these examples one can also point to the continued development of high-quality programming such as the HBO television series *The Sopranos, The Wire, Curb your Enthusiasm*, and *Six Feet Under* and the talents of many writers and producers on major networks to create such programs as *Everybody Loves Raymond, Cheers, Roseanne*, and *MASH*. Film, radio, and television have in a way proven that Arnold was correct: if one created a sound and challenging slate of shows and films, people will embrace them and elevate their tastes. Unfortunately, these modes of transmission also have proven that if one creates inferior programs, many people will embrace them, too.

From Iconic Images to Popular Culture Images

With the rise of popular culture as the primary producer of culture, it is important to understand the concept of image. This final section will discuss traditional notions of images; the ways in which these notions have shifted in meaning, including the rise of the digital image; and how images have become a form of style in popular culture.

As with understanding popular culture, one has to return to Plato to understand traditional notions of the image. Plato believed that the physical image was subordinate to the mental image or ideal. A graphic, or in Greek "Graphein," image is an imitation of an ideal that exists in its true, abstract form in the realm of thought. To Plato, the physical image was a poor and corrupt substitute for the true mental image. Graphein applies to anything that represents a physical mark, including a word, painting, etching, photograph, film, or any other mark used for expression. To discuss the difference between the mental image and the graphic image, Plato used the example of writing. For Plato, writing was a "pharmakon," meaning something used "to heal" and "to poison." Like all images, writing brought forth new explanatory powers to those who used it, but it also further removed people from the ideal. Plato believed that the only mode of communication that imitated the ideal of truth was speech, and any other form such as writing furthered removed the individual from the truth. In the case of writing, it poisoned the mind by creating a dependency on the written mark rather than promoting the development of the memory faculties within the brain.

Aristotle, Plato's student, held similar views. For Aristotle, a mental image was always present; thinking was impossible without it. As with his mentor, Aristotle subordinated any physical manifestation of the image to the mental realm.

Another tradition that places the mental or ideal over the physical image is religious iconology. The religious image is based on the notion of likeness; that is, the image is like a god. However, any physical or material likeness is a poor, corrupt manifestation of the celestial being. As Plato interpreted any written image as a poison, religious iconographers interpreted the physical manifestation of a spiritual being as a corruption. Spirits could manifest themselves as physical beings, but humans could never comprehend the splendor and beauty of the spirit because the physical characteristics never captured the true essence of the spirit.

The third tradition of the image is logical positivism. Within this tradition the image is a pure representation of nature and reality. The belief was that if a scientist captured nature through the use of a device within a laboratory, the image represented nature as it really existed in reality. In this tradition, snapshots or simulations of nature were not seen as momentary representations of what is possible in nature; they were seen as an unadulterated window into reality as it was happening. The laboratory device that captured the image was interpreted as neutral and the interpreter of the image was seen as a "ventriloquist" who merely reported what was there. Like the two traditions above, logical positivism privileged the abstract ideal that the image embodied. In these traditions, the image is interpreted as imitation that never creates reality or truth. With the rise of popular culture in the 19th century, these traditions would be challenged.

The major philosopher to challenge these traditions was Ludwig Wittgenstein. Wittgenstein concluded that the mental ideal should not be privileged because it was just another image. What mattered most in the discussion over abstract ideals and physical images was how these images represented meaning. For Wittgenstein, the only way in which images, mental or physical, came to mean anything was from shared experience. Therefore, the mental image could not be privileged because it was never a public image until spoken, written, or inscribed in another fashion so others could discuss and describe what the image might mean. It was during this social discussion of what an image means that reality and truth were constructed. Reality with Wittgenstein became a shared, or even popular, image.

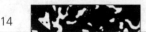

With the rise of literature as a dominant mode of communication, literary scholars privileged the image before Wittgenstein journeyed into the realm of images. However, most literary scholars began to privilege the image because they felt their mode of communication, the written word, was being threatened by the new image makers: photography and film. As the literary scholar J. Hillis Miller points out, numerous writers in the 19th and 20th centuries tried to dismiss the explanatory power of non-written images. Mark Twain, for instance, believed a picture meant "nothing without the label" (Miller, 1992, p. 62). Stéphane Mallarmé insisted that "words on the page have a performative power of evocation" (Miller, 1992, p. 67), while illustrations or any pictorial images distracted and diverted attention away from the real message of the author. Henry James interpreted the visual image as a danger to the text because the pictorial image would "usurp or darken the illuminating power of the text." To pacify this power to render words ineffective, James rationalized that illustrations were "in as different a medium as possible" (Miller, 1992, p. 68) and therefore "image and text echo one another at a safe distance" (Miller, 1992, p. 70).

The concerns raised by these literary giants reflected the reality that the Western world was becoming a visual culture and those people who illuminated our world through words were losing their power and status. They tried to combat this lost power by privileging the word over other images but, as pointed out above, writing, illustration, photography, films, and other forms of pictures come from the same word: Graphein, or "to write." While literary scholars were correct in recognizing the power of visual images to come, they missed the dynamic meaning-making process that requires both written and pictorial images. As Miller points out, written and pictorial images have a dialogical relationship that is at the same time similar but different. "[T]hey work the same way to produce meaning, as designs that are signs. A picture and a text juxtaposed will always have different meanings or logoi. They will conflict irreconcilably with one another, since they are different signs, just as would two different sentences side

by side, or two different pictures" (Miller, 1992, p. 95). Texts and pictorial images will always be images and they both construct meaning as images, but they will always construct this meaning in different ways. To take away one or privilege one over the other misses this dialogical relationship and denies everyone who creates and experiences (popular) culture the full joy of expression by any means (or images) possible. A society that prefers text over image or lives purely on pictorial images, as many do today, is an impoverished society.

Yet, W.J.T. Mitchell points out that **iconologists**, like literary scholars, have tried to privilege the text over the image, and as a result have created a disadvantage for academics who wish to understand societies, like the United States, that are dominated by the pictorial image. This privileging of the word over the image has led to what Mitchell refers to as the comparative method. This approach assumes that both the text and image share the common ability to express a meaning of mental image, and a text is better suited to do this most precisely and clearly. Visual images are too chaotic in their ability to secure meaning, while the written image can latch onto the meaning that best represents a thought.

To counteract this tendency to privilege the meaning-making abilities of the text over the image, Mitchell believes that one should not focus on the similarities between the text and image and then assume that the text is superior in capturing meaning, as comparative iconologists have done. Instead, one should focus on the materiality of each image. That is, texts and visual images are images but they convey meaning in different ways. Each image has its own potential to create meaning and one is not necessarily better than another. Each image embodies a different perspective necessary to maintaining a healthy and creative society that can see concerns and problems from different angles, lights, and meanings. Giving equal power and potential to the pictorial image can ensure that societies will have at their disposal all possible means to grapple with the problems of the day.

Iconologists

Mitchell's term to describe both traditional art and intellectual historians who researched the more traditional images of painting.

Mitchell's theory, which he now refers to as picture theory, has arrived on the scene at the perfect time, since Western societies have under-theorized the potential of the non-textual image even though the pictorial image dominates contemporary culture. Mitchell's theory stresses that we now have made what he calls "the pictorial turn." This turn is not "a return to naïve mimesis, copy, or correspondence theories of representation . . . , it is a complex interplay between visuality, apparatus, institutions, discourse, bodies, and figurality" (1994, p. 16). Instead of a retro theory that tries to recapture the glory of Platonism, religious iconography, or logical positivism, Mitchell's picture theory is a tool to help individuals navigate through the potential pitfalls of contemporary society. People who are able to attach meaning to textual and visual images will have the skill, power, and insight to name reality and control meaning. This power is simultaneously creative and potentially authoritarian. Given this potential, it is essential that people learn how to interpret and create the meaning of textual and visual images. This means people will have to recognize the power of popular culture images to create meaning. Those who refuse to recognize the power of popular culture will be labeled anachronistic and, even worse, irrelevant. At the same time, those who revel in the joy of popular culture without constructing their own meanings of the images are destined to be manipulated by those who construct meaning for them.

Ironically, at the very moment Mitchell has developed a pictorial theory, his efforts are being undermined by the digital image. To review, Mitchell's pictorial theory is based on the idea that each type of image (i.e., textual, photographic, and so on) adds something different to our ability to make meaning because each type of image has a different material basis (i.e., the word has the material form of a book, film has the form of celluloid, and so on). The digital image undermines this because now all images, textual or visual, have the same material basis: numerical. Fortunately for Mitchell, the power of the digital image to reduce all images to the same materiality does not undercut his important recognition that all types of images provide a different perspective of reality and therefore must be studied seriously and carefully without privileging one type over another. What the digital image does is change the ways in which we can construct different perspectives from images. Given this new power, it is important to discuss what a digital image is; how it creates numerous, never before visualized perspectives for creating new images; and what the digital image means for the study of popular culture.

Simply put, a digital image is an image reduced to numerical values. As Lev Manovich points out, "numerical representation turns media into computer data, thus making it programmable. And this indeed radically changed the nature of media." What numerical representation does is transform an image into a "finite number of pixels, each [pixel] having a distinct color or tonal value, and this number determines the amount of detail an image can represent" (Manovich, 2001, pp. 52–53). Media critics often proclaim that this process of numerical representation permits the user to copy the image without any loss in resolution, but since an image is reduced to pixels there is a loss of information or detail that one might find in other types of images. However, as Manovich notes, "technology has already reached the point where a digital image could easily contain much more information than anyone would ever want" (2001, p. 53). Therefore, in spite of any loss of information, the resolution of digital images still meets the visual and aesthetic needs of the viewer. The most pressing problem facing the creation of digital imagery is the large amount of space required to store these images. This storage issue explains why it is currently extremely expensive to use computer graphics in films and why streaming videos are still not common on home computers.

Despite its power to be infinitely copied, the digital image has an even greater strength. According to Manovich, a digital image's radical dimension is found in the concept called compositing. Compositing is the melding or "morphing" of layers or images to make them appear as if they were a single image. This ability cannot be found

in painting, traditional filmmaking, television production, or any form of popular culture. Compositing explains why most acting in films today is done in front of a blue screen. Actors perform their parts for the film, after which computer graphic artists add backgrounds and settings later in the production process. Compositing has also enabled film studios to make their own worlds by joining real-life acting with computer-generated characters and settings. There is no doubt that many of the films made today, from *Jurassic Park* to *The Matrix* trilogy or the latest *Star Wars* trilogy, could not have been made 15 years ago without compositing. Compositing makes it aesthetically possible and believable that a real actor can have a conversation with a computer-generated creature. Film has always been about making the unbelievable believable; compositing makes it easier for filmmakers to do this.

What compositing does is prove Mark Hansen's point that the digital image is much more than a new technique; it is a new "will to art." As a result, the digital image radically alters the relationship between humans and technology. Media scholar Friedrich Kittler suggests that the digital image is ushering in a new **posthuman** era in which humans are no longer necessary. For instance, films are moving to the point where human actors will no longer be needed except, perhaps, for voice generation, because convincing human-like images generated from computer images will be produced.

Posthuman traditionally means the "morphing" of humans with machines or the use of inorganic material to enhance or maintain the lives of organic material.

Hansen, however, suggests that Kittler goes too far in his proclamation of a posthuman age. Hansen does not question the dramatic impact the digital image has on popular culture. He recognizes that "the digital image explodes the frame [the materiality of film or television image] and thus creates a problematic of framing." That is, the celluloid frame is no longer needed to create a movie. However, "information always requires a frame [a way of seeing the world] . . . and . . . this framing function is ultimately correlated with the meaning-constituting and actualizing capacity of (human) embodiment" ("Cinema beyond Cybernetics," *Configurations*, volume 10, 2003, p. 89). Just as with Mitchell's picture theory, Hansen's theory of the digital image requires an acting, interacting, and interpreting human to create meaning for the image. Without the embodied human, there is no purpose for the digital image. The digital image serves as a continued reminder that we live in a new period in which popular culture plays a leading role in constructing reality, and those who understand the effects of popular culture in all dimensions of life will be better prepared to meet the challenges of the altered world that digital images are constructing, one pixel at a time.

The final point to make about images and popular culture is the image as style. So far, this chapter has discussed the image as a graphic mark or as a technological phenomenon. However, the term "image" also describes social status as well. Those who are able to capture the attention of the camera, even in negative ways, will be the political, cultural, and economic trendsetters. They will influence how people think, talk, dress, and interact with others. As Dick Hebdige notes, style is the "struggle between different discourses, different definitions and meanings . . . a struggle for possession of the sign which extends to even the most mundane areas of everyday life" (1989, p. 17). These stylistic struggles occur within popular culture; those who win will be the next generation of image-makers, superstars, and power-brokers. They will be the new cultural elite. This status as a cultural elite, however, is always fleeting. The management of images is constant, since trendsetters can be just a scandal away from losing their status. To understand this dimension of image as style, one has only to look at the latest troubles for Martha Stewart or Michael Jackson, two cultural trendsetters whose images have been tarnished and their income threatened. To counteract these negative images, Stewart and Jackson have taken to the airwaves to present their "side of the story," in the hope that their image in the public eye will revert to a positive one.

Defining Cultural Studies

The term "cultural studies" has numerous meanings. A general way to define cultural studies is as a multidisci-

plinary approach to the understanding of all dimensions of culture, from traditional notions to popular culture. It is multidisciplinary because no one field or method dominates. Some scholars, such as Andrew Ross and Greg Dimitriadis, adopt anthropological approaches; others, like N. Katherine Hayles and Donna Haraway, continue more traditional literary approaches; and Lawrence Grossberg and James Carey approach cultural studies from the field of communications. It is also multidisciplinary because almost every scholar "doing" cultural studies has a terminal degree in another field. For instance, Cary Nelson and Michael Bérubé have terminal degrees in literature programs; Hayles and Arkady Plotnitsky have degrees in math, science, and literature; Haraway is a biologist; and Stanley Aronowitz is a sociologist. There are institutional reasons as well why the field of cultural studies is interdisciplinary. Just as with other studies programs, administrators in institutions of higher learning have found it more cost-efficient to give their current faculty joint appointments in cultural studies rather than hire new faculty.

When defining the term cultural studies, one also has to recognize that the term implies a leveling of so-called high and low culture. The field of cultural studies does not assume that traditional culture is inherently superior to popular culture. At the same time, the traditional arts are not dismissed and ignored by scholars. Part of this belief that all forms of culture deserve equal attention is the commitment to explore the historical context in which cultures are created. The historical context helps contest the notion that great art or treasured canons come from genius or are anointed by God. If all cultural creations are bound within a historical context, then it is perfectly legitimate to assume that, if there are geniuses who create canonical treasures in traditional culture, similar creators can be found in popular culture as well.

Power is also a major component of any definition of cultural studies. If creative genius exists in all forms of culture, then the best way to explain why, until recently, artists within fields classified as popular culture were not recognized is the discriminatory nature of power. Prior to the 20th century, the authority and powers of the church, of landed aristocrats, of elitist critics, and of traditional artists were used to carefully defend their tastes from those of the "common people."

There is a geographical dimension to defining cultural studies as well. All culture is created within a local setting bound by its own historical context. However, as soon as that form of culture expands into other cultures, it takes on a global dimension that transforms the local cultures it comes from and is introduced to. There are two examples that demonstrate the relationship between the local and the global. First, there is the controversial exporting of American culture. Disney World, for example, was born within the specific context of a white man's Midwestern, middle-class culture and has since grown into a worldwide phenomenon symbolized by the image of Mickey Mouse and known by most children throughout the world. As Mickey Mouse was imported from the United States, it turned American culture into a global culture that threatened to undermine the indigenous cultures of other areas. For instance, instead of visiting a local vacation spot in their own countries, families might visit Disney World in Orlando or EuroDisney in France, thereby boosting the wealth of the Disney Corporation while threatening the travel industry of their own lands.

A second example is hip-hop music. Born out of traditional continental African music, American jazz, the blues, and urban life, hip-hop has become an international cultural movement that has reshaped the musical tastes, fashion styles, and language formations of millions of young people throughout the world. Anyone can walk the streets of Tokyo, Paris, Berlin, or Moscow and listen to the influence of hip-hop. Hip-hop has not been as destructive of indigenous cultures. It does threaten local musical cultures, but hip-hop's strength is its ability to co-opt different styles and sounds from indigenous cultures. As a result, when hip-hop enters into another culture it changes that culture without dominating it as much as Disney, MacDonald's, or Coke has.

There is also a national dimension to defining of cultural studies. To date, there have been attempts to distinguish various national cultural studies projects from other nations. There are American, British, Australian, French, and German cultural studies. While each of these approaches adopts similar theoretical traditions (i.e., poststructuralism), each offers its own distinct nationalist approach to local problems. For instance, Ien Ang's work in Australia is particularly focused on the role of Aborigines in the shaping of Australian culture. This is a distinct issue for Austrialians, just as the impact of Caribbean cultures on the British Isles is for England.

Finally, cultural studies can be simply defined as a common interest. James Carey, who claims to have introduced the term "cultural studies" to scholars in the United States, believes that cultural studies is "merely a coalition of people who had read some common books and had certain common concerns; scholars who shared a willingness to talk and a common stake in opening up academic discourse ("Reflections on the Project of (American) Cultural Studies," 1997, p. 6). Included in Carey's definition is an understanding that common concerns include a commitment to social justice and progressive ideals or the recognition that cultural concerns have an economic and political impact.

Glossary

Culture has numerous definitions. The text above presents two definitions (culture as proper tastes and culture as basic beliefs and values). Most scholars find the term elusive and multifaceted in meaning. The best definition comes from Raymond Williams, who defines culture as "a particular way of life which expresses certain meanings and values not only in art and learning, but also in institutions and ordinary behaviour" (*The Long Revolution,* 1961).

Cultural Capital is a term coined by the French sociologist Pierre Bourdieu. One can obtain cultural capital in two ways, either through education or birth. There are certain individuals who possess both and it is these people who have the most privilege in society. However, most cultural capital is

accumulated through education. In *Distinction: A Social Critique of the Judgement of Taste,* Bourdieu presents his detailed views on cultural capital and how it functions in society.

Kitsch is a German word that has been co-opted by the English language. In German it means cheap or trashy art, but in the United States it has come to signify trendy, accessible, and popular artwork.

Frankfurt School will be covered extensively in the next chapter. This group of sociologists, philosophers, anthropologists, and music scholars form one of the major traditions in 20th-century cultural studies.

Instrumentalism is a term used to describe the prevailing idea that an education ought not to necessarily cultivate the mind but prepare a person for a specific vocation. It is the mode of thinking that is pervasive in American universities today.

Americanization of Culture often implies the destruction of local, non-American cultures and the globalization of American culture as the only form of culture. See Fredric Jameson and Masao Miyoshi's edited volume, *The Culture of Globalization,* for a detailed writing on this meaning of Americanization of culture.

Iconologists is Mitchell's term to describe both traditional art and intellectual historians who researched the more traditional images of painting and those cultural scholars today, such as Mitchell himself, who are trying to broaden the more traditional study of images beyond painting and include popular culture images. In his own words, iconology is the "a study of the 'logos' (the words, ideas, discourse, or 'science') of 'icons' (images, pictures, or likenesses)" (1986, p. 1).

Posthuman traditionally means the "morphing" of humans with machines or the use of inorganic material to enhance or maintain the lives of organic material. The posthuman condition will be explained in more detail in Chapter 4.

Traditions of Popular Cultural Studies

Traditions in the study of popular culture are as varied and provocative as any other field of study. This chapter will discuss these traditions from the Frankfurt School to the United States traditions of cultural criticism that begin with Gilbert Seldes, to the Soviet tradition of Mikhail Bakhtin, to Marshall McLuhan, to the Birmingham Centre for Contemporary Cultural Studies.

The Frankfurt Tradition

The Frankfurt tradition is so named because of its intellectual connections to Frankfurt, Germany. During the Weimar Republic, numerous intellectuals from such diverse fields as sociology, musicology, anthropology, psychoanalysis, philosophy, and history created their own intellectual coterie that wished to move beyond and extend the work of Max Weber and Karl Marx. Unsatisfied by Weber's lack of revolutionary vision and Marx's primary focus on economic matters, the Frankfurt School sought to create a critical interpretation of society in general that moved from economics to the cultural realm. It was the

Critical Theory
according to the Frankfurt School, refers to the creation of a philosophical alternative to the dominant bourgeois capitalist mode of thinking.

Frankfurt School that introduced the term **"critical theory"** to the lexicon of 20th-century theoretical work. From a critical perspective, the Frankfurt School intellectuals, such as Theodore Adorno, Max Horkheimer, Leo Lowenthal, Herbert Marcuse, Walter Benjamin, and Siegfred Kracauer, developed in-depth studies of film, music, and everyday life as they related to capitalism, modernity, and fascism.

With the end of the Weimar Republic and the beginning of Nazi Germany, most of the Frankfurt intellectuals fled Germany. All of the intellectuals in this tradition were left-wing radicals, but many were also Jewish. Adorno, Horkheimer, and Marcuse, as well as most of the other Frankfurt School members, ended up in the United States, where they enhanced the intellectual atmosphere of American universities clear into the late 1960s. Adorno and Horkheimer joined numerous other German émigrés to found the New School of Social Research in New York City, which is now famous for its school of acting, directing, set design, and, James Lipton's program The Actor's *Studio* as seen on Bravo. Herbert Marcuse eventually landed at the University of California at Berkeley, where his book *One-Dimensional Man* became a cult classic for '60s counterculture. He has recently resurfaced as an intellectual celebrity because he was a professor of Ted Kuczynski, who also went by the name of "the Unibomber."

Walter Benjamin's plight was a little different. Most of the members of the Frankfurt School initially fled to England, but Benjamin was enamored with France. In 1933, when the threats of war were still distant, Paris seemed to be a safe choice. Benjamin believed Paris was the quintessential modern city. He wrote there and particularly enjoyed the Paris **arcade** scene. By 1939, however,

Arcade
for Benjamin and other early-20th-century inhabitants did not mean video games and pool tables. Arcades were similar to contemporary malls.

Paris was overrun by Nazis; Jews and radical thinkers were hunted down. In 1940, Benjamin tried to flee France through the Pyrenees. As his Spanish friends were ascending the mountains with a visa to enter neutral Spain, Benjamin panicked, believing that the Nazis were close to capturing him, and committed suicide.

When it comes to popular culture, the ideas embodied in the Frankfurt tradition are best expressed in Adorno and Horkheimer's "Culture Industry" and Walter Benjamin's "Art in the Age of Mechanical Reproduction." These essays, although from the same tradition, are as different as any two essays one can find on popular culture. Adorno and Horkheimer's essay casts popular culture as a pit of quicksand ready to ensnare the masses, while Benjamin's work sees more detail and potential in the popular medium.

Written in the shadow of the rubble left behind by World War II, "Culture Industry" is Adorno and Horkheimer's attempt to place the rise of popular culture within the perspective of fascist and neo-fascist societies. Popular culture, for Adorno and Horkheimer, is controlled and manipulated by the movie studio moguls while moviegoers, consumers, and fans are "statistics on research organization charts, and are divided by income groups" (Adorno and Horkheimer, 1998, p. 123). As part of the Nielsen ratings, people are manipulated to fit the genres and forms of popular culture created by media elites. From this blatant manipulation emerges a society in which "sustained thought is out of the question . . . no scope is left for the imagination" and people "react automatically" to what they see and hear in movie theaters or on television sets (Adorno and Horkheimer, 1998, p. 127). Every aspect of life is scripted, style is formulaic mediocrity, and image is propaganda. Advertising is the medium of the media elite and every commercial is a big lie in which "advertising becomes art and nothing else, just as Goebbels . . . combines them" (Adorno and Horkheimer, 1998, p. 163). As a result of this condition, the majority of people are rendered helpless, stuck in their recliners or theater seats unable to act and transcend the bland propaganda the media elite produce and call art. The culture industry for Adorno and Horkheimer is nothing but neo-fascism that would make Goebbels, the Nazi head of propaganda, proud.

Benjamin presented a starkly different perspective from Adorno and Horkheimer's view on popular culture. He did believe that popular culture was and could be

manipulated by the Nazis to mass-produce their propaganda. It is true that Hitler was a lover and manipulator of films (see *Triumph of the Will*), and all forms of popular media, especially radio, were used to sustain Nazi power in Europe. As Benjamin said, "Fascism is the introduction of aesthetics into political life" (1969, p. 241). Fascism is the use of popular culture to glorify the state and its leaders. However, Benjamin saw that popular culture had more potential beyond Nazi manipulation.

With the introduction of mechanical modes of reproduction, for Benjamin this primarily referred to photography and film, culture had been irrevocably changed. Mechanical reproduction created "aporios," or differences that cannot be reconciled but that co-exist in the realm of culture. With the rise of photography and film, the work of art lost its aura but gained a democratic flavor. The aura for Benjamin was a work of art's connection between the present and its historical roots. A person could visit a museum, see an original painting, enter into a relationship with that painting, and through that relationship understand its aura. Only a few people could do this, though; an original painting could share its aura only with those people who had time to enter into a relationship with it, who sought to understand its history, and, of course, who had permission to enter the museum. This was all lost when film and photography made works of art more accessible to people. Instead of going to a museum to see da Vinci's Mona Lisa on display, one could carry around a photograph or postcard of the painting. By the late 19th century, art came to the individual, which opened culture to more people. As a result, however, art lost its anchor to its past.

Mechanical reproduction disrupted the aura of art because it compressed time and space. The traditional work of art maintained its power through its slow but persistent movement through time. Before photography and film, every era of modern life brought about changes, but these rarely changed the work of art. With photography and film, speed and the compression of time became a dominant aspect of art. For Benjamin, "photography freed the hand of the most important artistic functions which henceforth devolved only upon the eye looking into a lens," while the filmmaker through the camera could capture "the images at the speed of an actor's speech." This new ability to "keep pace with speech" caused "the most profound change in [art's] impact upon the public" (Benjamin, 1969, p. 219). Art could be experienced in movie houses, newspapers, and magazines while "painting simply is in no position to present an object for simultaneous collective experience" (Benjamin, 1969, p. 234). Art was open to the consumption of the "masses," ushering in the beginning of popular culture and the end of high art.

This new era of mechanically reproduced art brought about changes between the artist and the audience in areas besides painting. For Benjamin, there are fundamental differences between theatrical stage actors and film actors, even if they both are performing the same material such as a Shakespeare play or a musical. When members of an audience view an actor on stage, they are watching a one-time performance that changes during each production. One can attend a Friday evening version of *Macbeth* on stage, and then catch the Saturday morning matinee and experience something completely different because the actors might have missed a line, entered the stage differently, or adjusted "to the audience during his performance" (Benjamin, 1969, p. 228). Film acting is completely different. Film actors are not performing in front of an audience; they perform for the camera. For Benjamin, the audience is absent. When the audience finally is permitted to experience the work of the film actor, the relationship has been defined by camera angles, editing, and splicing. With the camera as a mediator between the actor and audience, the film actor is transformed into an image, a "star" who is always different in person and larger than life on screen.

Cultural Criticism in the United States

While the Frankfurt tradition is well known and often cited in educational fields, the tradition of popular culture commentators in the United States is rarely mentioned in

Gilbert Seldes

(1893-1970) was one of the most important popular culture critics from the United States. His career spanned the rise of modern literary criticism as well as the development of all the major media of popular culture.

cultural studies and forgotten in education. When one is discussing cultural criticism in the United States, **Gilbert Seldes** is the person who has had the most impact. Seldes was a Harvard-trained literary critic who believed that popular culture should not be held up to the standards of so-called high culture but could produce masterful works of art on its own terms. As a graduate of Harvard in 1914, Seldes entered into the realm of American culture in a time when high culture was valued more than at any other time. Traditional cultural critics writing at the time saw absolutely no value in popular culture and firmly believed that only a few people in the United States were capable of understanding the meaning and purpose of high art and cultural criticism. Seldes fit easily into this realm of American life, serving as the editor of the literary magazine *The Dial*, which featured the work of T.S. Eliot, Sherwood Anderson, e.e. cummings, George Santayana, and Bertrand Russell. Seldes, however, was different. He believed that, just as high culture was an important part of American life, popular culture was important as well. The key to understanding popular culture from Seldes' perspective is to accept that it will never be high culture and never needs to be. In his classic book of essays on popular culture, *The Seven Lively Arts*, Seldes made this point clear. In reviewing the art of cinema, Seldes proclaimed that Mack Sennett's Keystone Kops reels were successful because they "had no pretensions to art" (1957, p. 13). The Keystone Kops created a "freedom of fancy, the wildness of imagination" and "let loose roaring . . . destructive, careless energy" (Seldes, 1957, p. 31). Seldes believed that one could also find this raw and imaginative greatness in comic strips such as "Krazy Kat" or the films of Charlie Chaplin.

To demonstrate the imaginative power of popular culture, Seldes established two major themes in his writings: the uncovering of popular culture and the immediacy of experiencing popular culture. Contrary to his colleagues, who viewed his work on the popular arts as discovery, Seldes believed that he was "uncovering," not "discovering," popular culture. For Seldes, the notion that one was

"discovering" popular culture was the height of pretension. Everyone knew about the power of vaudeville, Charlie Chaplin, Krazy Kat, jazz, and the Keystone Kops—"everyone, that is, except the critics" (Seldes, 1957, p. 4).

Embedded in his belief in the creative power of popular culture was a faith in the potential of people. In *The Public Arts*, Seldes wrote an open letter criticizing those people who proclaimed that the masses would accept anything that producers gave them. Seldes admitted: "In the long run the public does accept a lot of third rate stuff that it does not particularly care for . . . but that is no proof that they will not take anything better" (Seldes, 1956, p. 292). Creators and producers of popular art have to take it upon themselves to create that which elevates the taste of all. To do this, the cultural critic and popular artist have to realize that "the audience as boobs is satisfying to hucksters and to highbrows" who wish to weaken the demand for better products from the popular arts in order to distinguish their own tastes from those of the people. This might be acceptable to the aristocrat, but it is not "permanently acceptable to democrats" who, as critics, are entrusted with the charge to create the best possible forms of art as possible for all popular media.

Beyond questioning the cynicism and unfounded snobbery of many of his colleagues, Seldes believed he found what made popular culture different from the more traditional arts: immediate experience. "The popular arts," Seldes believed, "express the present moment, the instant mood" (Seldes, 1956, p. 286). This "instant mood" should not be confused with instant gratification or any other superficial term to degrade popular taste. Immediate experience was an important aspect of popular culture because from the 1910s to the 1950s vaudeville acts changed periodically, never to be seen again; films premiered and then disappeared from theaters; and live television shows were not shown as reruns until the 1960s and syndication was not common until the 1980s. Unlike a painting, which one could visit numerous times in a museum and enter into a relationship with, one could experience the popular arts only as long as they were available. Of course, this

has all changed with the development of subscription television (e.g., HBO), VCRs, DVDs, home videos, and syndication.

The concept of immediate experience also dealt with the way in which a person interacted with popular culture. Although not educated in musical criticism, Seldes wrote a few pieces on jazz. To understand jazz, one had to listen to it; one could not read about its power. "The analysis of jazz," Seldes wrote, "musically and emotionally, is not likely to be done in the spirit of jazz itself. There isn't room on the printed page for a glissando on the trombone, for the sweet sentimental wail of the saxophone. . . . The reason jazz is worth writing about is that it is worth listening to" (Seldes, 1957, p. 85). Like other forms of popular arts, jazz was powerful because one needed to use the senses to see, feel, and hear it.

There is another dimension of immediate experience. Seldes focused much of his critical attention on films because there is something special about viewing films that only music can rival. Films often inspire and uplift the emotions of those who watch them. Films create a feeling of inspiration that taps into what Gilles Deleuze called the "will to art." Today it is generally accepted that there is a connection between film-watching and creativity, but during Seldes' day to admit that emotions influenced the intellect was a risky proposition. Such an admission challenged the traditional Platonic viewpoint that clearly favored the intellect over any emotions, which Plato equated to opinion.

Popular culture critics in America who followed Seldes' tradition of criticism also tapped into the importance of immediacy. **Robert Warshow** was the most famous of those critics writing in the 1940s and 1950s. Although he valued the power of jazz, Warshow believed that one could understand the immediate experience of popular culture at its best in movies. Warshow believed that traditional film criticism slighted a "fundamental fact of the movies, . . . the actual, immediate experience of seeing and responding to the movies as most of us see them and respond to them" (Warshow, 2001, p. xl). To go see films

Robert Warshow

in spite of his movie reviews, is best known for his defense of comic books. In the late 1940s and 1950s Dr. Fredric Wertham was convinced that comic books were a major cause of juvenile crimes.

and experience them forced the critic out of the false dichotomy between so-called high and low culture. For Warshow there was no problem with false dichotomies; he had proven himself to be an astute critic of traditional culture and an unabashed lover of movies. As he noted in his essays, "I have felt my work to be most successful when it has seemed to display the movies as an important element in my own cultural life, an element with its own qualities and interesting in its own terms" (Warshow, 2001, p. xiii). It was this critical acceptance of popular culture that marked the early traditions of criticism in the United States.

There is one more United States tradition, embodied in the work of James Carey that should be addressed. Before this discussion, however, it is important to note the rise of the Soviet tradition of popular cultural studies, Marshall McLuhan's influence on cultural studies, and the Birmingham Centre of Contemporary Cultural Studies (CCCS). It is important to cover these traditions here for two reasons. First, like the work of Seldes and Warshow, the early work of cultural critics in the Soviet Union, Canada, and England were strongly influenced by traditional literary criticism; second, these traditions emerged chronologically before Carey's major work.

Cultural Criticism in the Soviet Union and Canada

The Soviet tradition centers around one person, Mikhail Bakhtin. Bakhtin was a literary critic who believed that the power of revolutionary change could be found in the nature of language and the culture of the people. His approach to language was dialogic or adhering to the belief that no one could control the meanings of words. For Bakhtin "there are no 'neutral' words and forms. . . . [L]anguage has been completely taken over, shot through with intentions and accents. . . . The word in language is half someone else's. It becomes 'one's own' only when the speaker populates it with his own intention" (Bakhtin, 1981, p. 293). By democratizing language, Bakhtin undermined anyone who wished to control the culture of words.

He recognized that anyone could try to act in an authoritative manner and attempt to control the meaning of words. However, any authoritative attempt to control meaning would stifle the life of words and the culture that lived through those words. Bakhtin's stance opened the door for scholars to value the language of popular culture as a form of knowing and meaning.

From his dialogical approach to meaning, Bakhtin believed that one could understand the vitality of a society through the ways in which the general population created meaning in everyday life. Stemming from this belief, Bakhtin began his major study of the 16th-century scholar Antonie Rabelais. In *Rabelais and His World*, Bakhtin explored how the vitality of a society could be found in the everyday traditions of people. Bakhtin discussed the role of **carnivalesque** fesitivals, such as Mardi Gras, to undermine the authority of royalty and the church. During these festivals people would mimic and lampoon kings, queens, and church figures in a manner that was grotesque (i.e., use of foul language, crude displays of bodies, and gluttonous eating habits). Bakhtin noted that it was through these grotesque actions that people questioned the tastes and culture of those in power and sent a clear message that they believed all people were equal. Bakhtin found parallels between Rabelais and his world of 16th-century Europe and the "revolutionary" Soviet Union of the 1930s. Bakhtin maintained that for people to uphold revolutionary values they had to abandon all authoritative claims to language and culture, as the people of Rabelais' world did. For his efforts to create an open language and dynamic popular culture, Bakhtin spent much of his life during Stalin's reign in exile away from the intellectual center of Moscow.

Marshall McLuhan is by far the most famous scholar interested in popular culture. Educated in England at Cambridge and the Centre of Contemporary Cultural Studies, McLuhan spent most of his academic career teaching in Canada. He is most famous for his dictum "the medium is the message," which is often cited but rarely explained. McLuhan believed that the medium was the message "because it is the medium that shapes and con-

Carnivalesque

a term used to describe the use of popular culture to question dominant cultural forms and to create anarchical forms of culture that demonstrate little regard for tastes and decorum.

trols the scale and form of human association and action" (McLuhan, 1964/1994, p. 9). McLuhan realized that what changed modern 20th-century society was the reality that almost every experience was mediated through some form of mass communication. These forms, whether film, television, radio, or the telephone, transformed how people interacted with the world and, more important, who people were, both psychologically and physiologically. It is his insistence that humans were altered physiologically that makes McLuhan an intriguing scholar. McLuhan believed that all media were either hot or cold. A hot medium, such as film or radio, is that which "extends one single sense in 'high definition.' High definition is the state of being well filled with data" (McLuhan, 1964/1994, p. 22). A cold medium, such as the telephone or television, contains less data in its resolution. This reduction of the relationship between humans and machines to an information (data) flow, McLuhan believed, altered humans in a profound way. As he noted, "any invention or technology is an extension or self-amputation of our physical bodies, and such extension also demands new ratios and new equilibriums among the other organs and extensions of the body" (McLuhan, 1964/1994, p. 45). What he meant by this statement was that when we watch a film, for instance, our sight and hearing are enhanced; this enhanced ability to see and hear beyond our normal capabilities alters our whole body. The technology of film acts like a prosthetic, altering the whole human condition right down to the nervous system and consciousness. McLuhan was the first person to recognize the cultural ramifications of information technology, which transforms its users into posthumans.

The Birmingham Tradition

The Birmingham Centre for Contemporary Cultural Studies is by far the most famous and influential tradition in popular cultural studies. Although it is unclear who created the term "cultural studies," the Birmingham school is often given credit. Prior to the appearance of the term

"cultural studies" in the Birmingham school, most people interested in popular culture did not proclaim that they did cultural studies. The Frankfurt scholars saw themselves as social and political critics; writers from the U.S. tradition described themselves as literary scholars and critics who happened to focus some of their attention on popular culture; and Bakhtin viewed his work as literary criticism. This is why the term "popular cultural studies" has been used in this book up to this point. From now on, however, the term "cultural studies" will be used. But I do not want to give the impression that I support the idea that the Birmingham school invented the term "cultural studies." There are plenty of histories that attribute the Birmingham school with coining this phrase. For instance, in their introduction to "the new wave" of cultural studies, Henry Jenkins, Tara McPherson, and Jane Shattuc (2003) suggest that the Birmingham School created the phrase "cultural studies," as does Nadine Dolby in her introductory essay for a *Harvard Educational Review* (2003) issue on popular culture. Handel Kashope Wright contests this idea. Wright (1998) locates the beginnings of cultural studies at the Kamiriithu Community Education and Cultural Centre in Limuru, Kenya. It is noteworthy, too, that many scholars associated with the Birmingham School, such as Stuart Hall, Angela McRobbie, and Paul Willis, dismiss the idea that the Centre for Contemporary Cultural Studies invented the term or were the first to "do" cultural studies.

The first generation of scholars, Raymond Williams, Richard Hoggart, and **E.P. Thompson** at the Birmingham School, were indeed more traditionalists in the mold of Seldes, Bakhtin, or Warshow—cultural critics educated in the traditions of literature who happened to focus on popular culture. It was not until the rise of the second generation of scholars, with Stuart Hall serving as a bridge between the two generations, that cultural studies as it is defined today dominated academic interest in popular culture.

Even though the first Birmingham scholars were more literary—and, in Thompson's case, historical—their work is monumental and worth mentioning in some detail.

E.P. Thompson

(1924-1993) was an English historian whose most famous work, The Making of the English Working Class (1966), charted the rise and creation of working-class culture in 18th-century England.

Hoggart and Williams were the first leaders in the Birmingham School. Educated under Leavis (see Chapter 1) at Cambridge, Hoggart and Williams both received a traditional literary education with a critical and commentative approach to scholarship. With their first major books, *The Uses of Literacy* for Hoggart and *Culture and Society* for Williams, they questioned this traditional approach to literary scholarship and incorporated a broader understanding of what the term "culture" means.

Hoggart in *The Uses of Literacy* was not interested in how those with so-called aristocratic tastes define culture. Instead, he wanted to chart the ways in which working-class cultures evolved over the first 50 or so years of the 20th century. Hoggart worked from the common observation at that time that England was moving from a deeply divided, class-based society to a classless order through what scholars referred to as a "bloodless revolution." If England no longer had class divisions, what one class did they become? Whose tastes did they adopt? Fitting in the traditional scholarly mold, Hoggart focused his attention on magazines and people who read them. He concluded that for magazines to survive, they needed a broad base of readers that one specific class could not support. Therefore, magazines transcended class tastes while inviting members of different classes to subscribe to their journal. The result of creating a broad-based readership was the creation of a consuming class. Hoggart did not necessarily embrace this shift to a consuming class, however. The creation of a mass culture was pushing England into a society of conformists who shared the same bland and shallow tastes. Hoggart concluded that "we seem to be reading fewer different papers, but yet to be reading a greater number; to be reading more often, that is the same papers as each other." (Hoggart, 1957, p. 259). The results of reading more of the same for Hoggart were devastating. Not only were working class cultures disappearing, but life as the British knew it was as well. Mass culture was for Hoggart was "in the end what D. H. Lawrence described as 'anti-life' . . . a seeking of material possessions, equality as a moral leveling and freedom as the ground of endless

irresponsible pleasure" (Hoggart, 1957, p. 263). Through his research, Hoggart had stumbled upon an important theme that has characterized the last 60 years in the Western world: to live is to consume and to have fun at any cost, even if it means working at a meaningless job in order to enjoy two weeks out of the year during vacation time.

Williams, in his work, sought to define what the term "culture" meant for the past two centuries within the context of industry, democracy, and the arts. Traditional in scope, Williams focused his attention on literary figures who dominated the intellectual scene since the early 1800s, including Matthew Arnold, T.S. Eliot, and Thomas Carlyle—hardly ardent supporters of anything other than the most stringent notions of culture. Like Hoggart, Williams' conclusions were more important than his historical analysis. Williams concluded that culture was undergoing a revolutionary change in meaning because of the dramatic technological changes England experienced. Modern modes of communications existed throughout the period Williams covered in the book. However, Williams pointed out, forms of communication that were only for the few in the 19th century now are constructed for the masses. Mass communication has come to dominate the way in which people communicate and see the world. The shift to mass communications presents interesting problems for a democracy. When a person or group attempts to communicate with others there is always the potential for exploitation, or the presenting of only one perspective. This exploitation can either be dictatorial or educational. As a result, Williams concluded that in the new world of mass communication "the objection . . . is not to telling anyone anything. It is a question of how one tells them, and how one would expect to be told oneself" (Williams, 1958, p. 314). That is, mass communication is a matter of informing people and making sure they are receiving information that creates opportunities for them to elevate their material and intellectual conditions. To do otherwise would be to abuse the technology of mass communication. As will be evident in the discussion of televi-

sion in Chapter 3, this issue shaped William's research throughout his career.

The most famous and influential scholar from the Birmingham School was Stuart Hall. While Hoggart's and Williams' influence was waning at CCCS, Hall's influence remained steady. Hall's academic career began when Hoggart and Williams were publishing their first works in the late 1950s and his influence continues to be felt today, even though the Centre for Contemporary Cultural Studies disbanded in 2001. Hall's intellectual strength was in his ability to comment on current theories as they might apply to the study of popular culture. He was a self-described "reluctant **post-structuralist**." Hall was one of the first theorists to recognize that traditional Marxism was reductionist in its insistence that all social factors should be reduced to economic factors. Hall believed that even though economic factors and social inequalities could not be ignored in order to create a more progressive and socialist society, culture could not be ignored either. In trying to avoid reductionist Marxism without abandoning its political agenda, Hall adopted **Antonio Gramsci**'s notion of hegemony. Hegemony is the belief that modern societies do not maintain power through brute force but through persuasion. If power is not a matter of military might or police brutality, then how is power maintained? Gramsci concluded that power was maintained through institutions of culture such as schools and mass media. The power elite formed power blocs consisting of people from all social classes who believed that the social order as it existed was the best form of government no matter how much certain groups might suffer. Schools and mass media outlets became conduits through which people were persuaded that those in power were the legitimate heirs to rule. Of course, this hegemonic process is never complete or settled. As a result, different power blocs are constantly waging "wars" of persuasion through various institutional outlets offering up alternative visions of what the world can be. It was the ways in which mass mediums were used hegemonically that interested Hall in popular culture.

Within the realm of popular culture, Hall's most

Post-structuralistm refers to the influence of French theorists such Jacques Derrida, Giles Deleuze, Michel Foucault, and Jean François Lyotard on progressive and socialist thought since the 1960s. Post-structuralism is the theoretical belief that no theory can provide the final answer or any structural laws that govern societies.

Antonio Gramsci (1891-1937) was an Italian Communist who wrote much of his most famous works in prison.

important concept was articulation. What Hall had in mind with this term were two things. First, he accepted the more traditional notion of articulation: to articulate, utter, or speak. Second, "we also speak of an 'articulated' lorry (truck) . . . where the front (cab) and back (trailer) can, but not necessarily, be connected to one another. . . . An articulation is thus the form of the connection that can make a unity of two different elements, under certain conditions" (Grossberg, 1996, p. 141). The elements are the ever-changing conditions of everyday life and the certain conditions are the material, economic, and social conditions through and by which people live. Hall was interested in how these forces are articulated in popular culture and in politics.

Hall's eclectic theoretical ambitions are also embodied in the term "hybridity," which is a crucial term to understand popular culture. Hall was born in Jamaica and of African descent. Although educated in England and a leader in higher education, Hall never felt at home in England. He always viewed himself as a **post-colonial** intellectual, one whose home was always elsewhere. Hall used this lack of roots in England to expose nationalistic and xenophobic tendencies in English higher education specifically and in society in general, which classified in stringent ways who was considered English and who was not.

Post-colonial or Post-colonialism

an intellectual and political movement to think about non-Western life outside the established parameters of Western European tastes.

Hall's theories and works were tremendous catalysts to create a new area of cultural studies that completely broke from the traditions of literary criticism. While Hoggart and Williams felt an obligation to connect with traditional notions of culture in their work, there are no visible signs of this tradition in the second generation of cultural studies scholars who hail from the Birmingham School. As a result of this freeing from the traditions of literary criticism, the work of the second generation of cultural studies scholars in England is as diverse and impressive as any other field in the academic world.

Dick Hebdige's work is of considerable note. Hebdige has done work on style, music, and subcultures in Great Britain and the United States. Chapter 3 will further discuss Hebdige's contribution to style and music; therefore, this chapter will concentrate on his notion of subculture. By "subculture," Hebdige does not mean "subordinate" or "inferior" to a dominate culture. In fact, in his seminal work, *Hiding in the Light*, he demonstrates how subcultures exist right in front of dominant cultures without being detected (and regulated). This ability to exist without regulation gives subcultures a great deal of power to create the meaning of popular culture. In fact, one can look at the facets of popular culture and see that it is usually a subculture that is setting the trends and defining what is important. One needs to look no further than the impact of hip-hop in the United States. Hip-hop has done more to define youth cultures than anything dominant adult cultures have constructed. Hip-hop has defined fashion, sports, advertising, television, films, magazines, and language. Certain people within dominant cultures have tried to regulate and sanction it, but their failure to control hip-hop shows how inept and impotent dominant cultures are and how powerful subcultures are.

Angela McRobbie is another scholar from the Birmingham School whose impact has been great. One of the first scholars, along with Charlotte Brunsdon, to demonstrate in the 1970s that the CCCS had ignored feminism and women's issues, McRobbie has built a stellar academic career creating innovative work centering on women in culture. Her latest work deals with the revitalization of the British fashion industry and how women are playing a key role in this demanding and competitive economic sector. McRobbie has constructed theoretical ways to understand that, when it comes to women, economic issues such as shopping are cultural endeavors (i.e., window shopping as a leisure activity), and that cultural endeavors (i.e., consumption) are economic issues (i.e., grocery shopping for the family or for the family they work for) as well. The area of cultural studies is often criticized for not being practical enough politically. However, McRobbie's work demonstrates how cultural studies can inform progressive policies.

Paul Gilroy is another Birmingham scholar who is

currently teaching sociology at Yale University. Following Hall, Gilroy is interested in post-colonial issues in Great Britain and beyond. In his work he has demonstrated how English citizens who are of non-European descent have to constantly maintain a double consciousness. Gilroy attacks the tendencies to essentialize the "other." Just as there is no real "Englishman" who is the purest symbol of Great Britain, Gilroy contests there is no pure "other" who is the epitome of what Great Britain should not be. Non-European English people are in a constant state of identity negotiation. For example, an English citizen who is originally from Jamaica or who has Jamaican descendents is constantly reminded that he or she is neither Jamaican nor British. These people, therefore, are constantly inventing who they are, what their roots mean, and what it means to be an English citizen. Out of his studies Gilroy hopes to create a new understanding of what it means to be a citizen that is simultaneously inclusive of non-European peoples and yet, at the same time, exclusive enough for these peoples to construct connections to their own past that is not dictated or dominated by white Europeans.

The last example of the Birmingham School, Lawrence Grossberg, serves as a segue back to the University of Illinois tradition of cultural studies in the United States and the work of James Carey. Grossberg was educated at both the University of Illinois and Birmingham University in England. Grossberg's contributions to theory are impressive. His most important theoretical contribution to cultural studies is his use of articulation to understand the **affective** dimensions of popular culture. Grossberg has written about rock-and-roll music and the rise of conservatism in the United States. When he began his work, he wanted to understand how conservatives were able to co-opt the anti-establishment undercurrent of rock music to further strengthen their hold on power. That is, how were conservatives able to articulate their views in a way that encouraged rockers such as Ted Nugent or Bon Jovi and their fans to support conservative causes? Besides using articulation to explain this, Grossberg introduced the affective domain. For Grossberg

Affective
best described through the words of Lawrence Grossberg in his 1992 work We Gotta Get Out of This Place. The affective "is closely tied to what we often describe as the 'feeling' of life. . . . Such 'feeling' is a socially constructed domain of cultural effects" p. 80.

the affective is a superficial connection to popular culture that gives fans a sense of belonging, especially in a culture in which so many people feel alienated from the democratic process. Popular culture with its affective (emotional) bonds has served as a substitute for democracy. The affective goes a long way to explaining why most people know every player on their favorite sports team and proudly wear the team's logo while they are hard-pressed to name their own congressperson.

The last tradition to be addressed in this chapter is embodied in James Carey's work. This tradition is important to note because it offers a distinct alternative pathway to cultural studies. Every tradition and individual mentioned above, with the exception of Grossberg and some members of the Frankfurt tradition, were either directly linked to a literature department or trained in traditional literary studies. Carey and the Illinois tradition have their roots in the field of communications. One can trace these roots to Walter Lippmann and his work *Public Opinion* (1922) and see that the field of communication is a distinctly United States creation. In his contribution to the field of cultural studies, Carey introduces the work of American pragmatism and sociology. Carey's ideas are deeply influenced by the work of John Dewey, C. Wright Mills, Edward Shils, and, of course, Lippmann. Embedded in the ideas of these thinkers are progressive ideals similar to any of the cultural studies scholars from the Frankfurt or Birmingham traditions. For Carey, cultural studies is an extension of progressive politics. As he notes, "If we follow Dewey, it will occur to us that problems of communication are linked to problems of community, to problems surrounding the kinds of communities we create and in which we live" (1992, p. 33). The work of cultural studies, therefore, is about democratic politics and fostering the principles of equality through the ways in which we communicate with each other. How open and free our popular outlets of expression are will determine to a great extent how free a people we are. What does this say about our contemporary reality when the majority of our popular communication outlets are controlled by an oli-

garchy of corporations?

Carey's contribution to the field of cultural studies does not end with the infusion of communication studies into the study of popular culture. Carey is a sharp critic and commentator of French thought. Commenting on the merger of British cultural studies and French thought, Carey believes it "has been . . . a deeply deforming episode" (1997, p. 15). Unlike other critics, who will be discussed in Chapter 4, Carey applauds the commitment that British and French scholars have made to social justice and he understands the theories behind post-structuralism. However, he believes such a move toward post-structuralism is a mistake because in the United States the struggle with social scientific positivism over the university and social policy is not complete. If the positivists are to "win out" over progressive cultural studies scholars, the university will become a stale and irrelevant place. Academics will dilute their minds with delusions of objectivity and value neutrality, and the goal of scholars will become the search for grants to conduct research that does not alter the basic structure of an American society that is drifting too far from its democratic roots. Carey believes that cultural studies needs to maintain its connections to the social sciences in order to push for the creation of progressive social policies.

Glossary

Critical Theory, according to the Frankfurt School, refers to the creation of a philosophical alternative to the dominant bourgeois, capitalist mode of thinking. The Frankfurt School was interested in offering a critique of capitalism while offering the proletariat and intellectual the means to create an alternative society based on equality and intellectually high standards. Today, the term "critical theory" is often reduced to critical-thinking skills that have nothing to do with social transformation and revolution and everything to do with getting a job and accepting the status quo.

Arcade for Benjamin and other early-20th-century inhabitants did not mean video games and pool tables. An arcade was similar to contemporary malls, except that arcades were

located in the heart of a city where people shopped in a variety of stores and mingled with other urban citizens.

Gilbert Seldes (1893–1970) is without a doubt one of the most important popular culture critics from the United States. His career spans the rise of modern literary criticism as well as the development of all the major mediums of popular culture. Seldes wrote numerous literary and stage reviews as well as screenplays for motion picture studios and later television studios. He was the first television programmer for CBS and later the first Dean of Annenberg School of Communications at the University of Pennsylvania.

Robert Warshow, in spite of his movie reviews, is best known for his defense of comic books. In the late 1940s and 1950s, Dr. Fredric Wertham was convinced that comic books were a major source for juvenile crimes. Warshow believed such views were naïve because they ignored other major problems in the lives of young people. Warshow believed Wertham's claims were unfounded because it was too much of a leap in logic to conclude that since young people read about violence and crimes in comics they would subsequently commit violent acts and crimes themselves.

Carnivalesque is a term used to describe the use of popular culture to question dominant cultural forms and to create anarchical forms of culture that demonstrate little regard for tastes and decorum. Today, the best example of a carnivalesque approach to culture are television shows such as *The Jerry Springer Show* or, an even better example, the sitcom *Roseanne*.

E.P. Thompson was an English historian whose most famous work, *The Making of the English Working Class* (1966), charted the rise and creation of working class culture in 18th-century England.

Post-structuralism refers to the influence of French theorists such as Jacques Derrida, Giles Deleuze, Michel Foucault, and Jean François Lyotard on progressive and socialist thought since the 1960s. Post-structuralism is the theoretical belief that no theory can provide the final answer on any structural laws that govern societies. In place of theoretical certainty and universal laws, post-structuralism constitutes a body of theories that envision the world both semantically and materially open to an unlimited number of possibilities that can be put into action. These possibilities can be progressive, repressive, or benign. How the meanings of these possibilities play out is not determined by any structural laws but by everyday interaction and as these interactions change, so

do the possibilities for theorizing. Hall reluctantly accepted the theories of post-structuralism because he saw that traditional Marxist theory was no longer providing any insights into the changes that were occurring in Europe, but he still believed that post-structuralism did not offer the political hope that was necessary to change the economic and social order. Hall feared that post-structuralism was academic jargon that disconnected the university from the public.

Antonio Gramsci (1891–1937) was an Italian Communist who wrote much of his most famous works in prison. With the rise of Mussolini, Gramsci was considered too dangerous to live free and too popular to be executed, so he spent much of his adult life in prison.

Post-colonial or **Post-colonialism** is an intellectual and political movement to think about non-Western life outside the established parameters of Western European tastes. In this sense of the term, the "post" refers to the need to create new traditions or reconnect to older non-Western traditions. The term is also used as a reminder that no matter how liberated current post-colonial peoples are from their former imperial repressors, the lingering effects of colonialism (i.e., economic dependency and intellectual dominance) still exist.

Affective is best described through the words of Lawrence Grossberg in his 1992 work *We Gotta Get Out of This Place.* The affective "is closely tied to what we often describe as the 'feeling' of life. . . . Such 'feeling' is a socially constructed domain of cultural effects. Some things feel different from others, some matter more or in different ways than others. The same experience will change drastically as its affective investment or state changes. . . . Affect operates across all of our senses and experiences, across all of the domains of effects which construct daily life." The affective is an emotional investment that varies from person to person and situation to situation, depending on how much we feel connected to an issue (e.g., abortion), a thing (e.g., sports team), or another person (e.g., pop star).

Films, Television, Music, and Fan Cultures

Almost everything in this century that people come to know is through some form of mediation. Traditionally, it was believed that each individual was directly connected to reality. Plato believed that the spoken word, when spoken in one's own voice, was a representation of an independent reality. Scientists after Isaac Newton believed in the correspondence theory of truth or the idea that, when a scientist conducted an experiment in the laboratory, his or her findings were representative of what actually existed in nature. This belief is what Donna Haraway calls "modest witnessing." The modest witness "is the legitimate and authorized ventriloquist for the object world [nature], adding nothing from his mere opinions, from his biasing embodiment. And so he is endowed with the remarkable power to establish the facts" (Haraway, 1997, p. 24). In the world of the modest witness, reality was represented by objective criteria that established certain facts about the world.

Today, few believe in Plato's ideals or the modest witness. Most people accept that we can know only the world

through some form of mediation. As Peter McLaren writes about this current state of affairs: "[W]e can have direct experience of the world but that knowledge about it is only possible in a secondary sense through semiotic systems" (McLaren, 1995, pp. 100–101). These semiotic systems of representation take the form not only of languages but also of films, television programs, and musical lyrics. Whatever form systems of representation take, they "re-present" reality. For instance, television newscasts take what happened during the day; reduce these events to 30 or 60 minutes, add images, graphics, and interviews; and call it reality. How newsmakers handle this process of reduction shapes how viewers interpret the world. Another example is filmmakers. Filmmakers take a fiction or non-fiction script, shoot the scenes from numerous angles, add computer graphics, edit the numerous reels, and call it a cinematic story. Both of these media serve as conduits into how we see and interpret reality. As we enjoy a film or listen to a news story, reality is being shaped before our very eyes.

If we always experience reality through a medium, what does it mean to "re-present" reality? 1) It means abandoning any notion that information can be filtered in a non-ideological or unbiased way. As long as humans exist, there will be bias. 2) "Re-presentation" implies that meaning or truth is never natural in its existence but constructed, and these constructions are situated within a historical context shaped by those who control the medium. 3) All re-presentations are generative. That is, all images, including words, that pass through this book have to be interpreted. For instance, viewers of films or television programs are not passive receivers but active meaning-makers. This requires viewers to be able to "read" visual images. "Meaning is a dialogue," Stuart Hall suggests, "always only partially understood, always an unequal exchange" (Hall, 1997, p. 4). It is unequal in terms of who creates the images we read, and unequal in terms of how each individual defines important information to glean from a broadcast, film, book, or music video. 4) Re-presentation implies that the re-presenting process does not merely pertain to words but to images from photographs, film frames, television screens, CDs, and computer graphics. They are all material forms of transmitting information and potential meaning. In this process of re-presenting information, individuals are bombarded with bits and bytes of potential facts, and each of us has to decide which information is important for us to achieve our individual goals each day. As a result of this meaning-making process through a re-presenting of information, it is fair to suggest that although we live in the same world, we shape the world differently depending on how we interpret information. It is also fair to assert that films, television, and music are the primary means in which people construct their reality.

This chapter will cover these three important modes of re-presenting reality: first film, then television, and finally music. In each case, this chapter will discuss how these media changed the way we see the world and how these forms have come to shape our realities. The chapter will also discuss fan cultures, from spectators to poachers and how people construct meaningful lives from their media of re-presentation.

Films

Most media scholars agree that any new medium or mode of representation is not a radical break from more established media. Film is no exception. When discussing the aesthetics and technology of film or cinema, early thinkers viewed it as an extension of photography.

French film critic André Bazin viewed photography as "aimed against death" (Bazin, 1967, p. 9). Photography captured a person or place in an image, overcoming "the conditions of time and space that govern it" (Bazin, 1965, p. 14). When cinema was fully developed in the late 1890s, the limitations of photography to cheat death were revealed. What photography lacked was the ability to capture movement. The image in the photo may have overcome mortal limitations, but it was frozen in time. Unable to move, it was a still image. Film, however, changed this limitation.

Movement, or the ability to capture the motion of people through time, is what distinguishes film from other popular culture media. Movement also connects film to later technological developments, such as television, video cameras, and virtual reality. Early film spectators were enthralled with cinema's ability to capture reality. The urban myth surrounding the Lumiere brothers' film premiere in 1895 is that people were convinced the train they viewed on the screen was really coming at them and fled the theater. This ability to capture movement was what gave cinema its popular name: movies. Even when directors such as Fritz Lang, Friedrich Murnau, and Ernst Lubitsch introduced **expressionism** and **montage** techniques into film production, people were convinced of the realism of the film. Again Bazin captured what people thought about early films when he wrote: "In their imaginations they saw the cinema as a total and complete representation of reality" (Bazin, 1967, p. 20). The realism of film encouraged the art historian Edwin Panofsky to proclaim that "today there is no denying that narrative films are not only 'art' . . . but also, besides architecture, cartooning, and 'commercial design,' the only visual art entirely alive" (Panofsky, 1995, p. 94). This might seem strange to contemporary moviegoers who do not have the same belief in the realism of film, but a contemporary comparison to realism in early film and today is virtual reality. Where people 100 years ago might have seen reality in celluloid, people today have the same opinion when it comes to virtual reality. Realism has not disappeared in the imaginations of people; only the technology has.

Of course this belief in cheating death and suspending the imagination in order to believe that what cinematographers captured on film was real has limitations and conditions. The new media critic Lev Manovich contends that for film to be realistic the screen has to act like a prison of the mind. The spectators of the film must remain captured in their seats; once they divert their attention from the screen, the effect disappears and reality, with all its physical laws, returns. However, for those brief moments that we experience films we are part of what Panofsky

Expressionism

a 20th-century art movement based on the distortion of images and color.

Montage

a style adopted from photography and painting that places more than one image into a frame to signal to the filmgoer the multiple parts that make up the whole film.

called the "dynamization of space," in which the spectator "is in permanent motion as [his or her] eye identifies itself with the lens of the camera, which permanently shifts in distance and direction (Panofsky, 1995, p. 98)."

The ability to captivate the spectator in a feeling of perpetual motion opens up another interesting phenomenon of film. Film places the viewer in a paradoxical position between poles of distance and proximity, and absence and presence. For film philosopher Stanley Cavell, movies overcome the problem of distance through visuals and sound. Like the painting, telegraph, and photograph, films reduce the distance in both time and space between the image and the viewer. In film, Cavell contends, the viewer sees things that are not present. The viewer was not there when the film was made nor when the actors prepared numerous takes on the set. Yet there the viewers are, projecting themselves into the film, and there the actors are, sitting, standing, running, or talking right in front of the viewers. The movie projector has overcome the problem of distance, bringing far-off lands into the local theater and, now with VCRs and DVDs, into the living room. This ability of the projector is what led Benjamin (see Chapter 2) to conclude that the arts have changed as we no longer have a relationship with the artists but with the camera. It is the camera that mediates our relationship with our favorite movie stars. The camera permits us to overcome distance and visit any actor we wish to. Cavell puts the paradox of proximity and distance this way: "The audience in a theater can be defined as those to whom the actors are present while they are not present to the actors" (Cavell, 1971, p. 25). The American movie critic Parker Tyler put it this way: "The fundamental eye trickery that is a genius of the camera—you see the object, yet it isn't there" (Tyler, 1947, p. xv).

This ability to overcome distance, present the illusion of reality, and suspend mortality are some of the reasons why film was an instant hit with 20th-century people and why it continues to thrive. Another reason for its early popularity was the ability of filmmakers to borrow from other media. That is, film was embraced because it was

merely another extension of forms of established entertainment. Mariam Hansen suggests that "the Wild West, minstrel, and magic shows, the burlesque, the playlet, the dance number, pornographic displays, acrobatics, and animal acts—all supplied the cinema with subject matter, performance conventions, and viewer expectations" (Hansen, 1991, p. 29). Most actors in early films were veterans of other forms of entertainment. Charlie Chaplin and Oliver Hardy were from vaudeville and traveling pantomime shows; Marie Dressler and Douglas Fairbanks from live theater; Lon Chaney from clown and dance acts. Today, there is similar movement but in both directions. Actors come from Broadway, the comedy circuit, or television and create films, while others move from making films to acting in Broadway plays or even in off-Broadway shows throughout the United States.

Directors were always borrowing from other media and from each other to transform and advance filmmaking. Lang, Murnau, and Lubitsch borrowed from art to create their sets; Sergei Eisenstein drew his inspiration from D.W. Griffith and Russian art. This tradition continues as Philip Jackson, director of the *Lord of the Rings* trilogy, borrows from computer graphics—as the next generation of filmmakers will certainly borrow from Jackson.

From a screenwriter's perspective, borrowing was and still is a must. Numerous famous films were based on adaptations from novels. For instance, *Gone with the Wind*, Greta Garbo's *Anna Karenina*, F.W. Murnau's *Nosfuratu*, and Walt Disney's *Snow White* and *Cinderella* were adapted from literary pieces. Adaptations from novels are still commonplace today, as witnessed by the success of *The Talented Mr. Ripley*, *Jaws*, *Cold Mountain*, *The Color Purple*, *Beloved*, and Oliver Stone's *JFK*. There always have been original screenplays written for film and now there is a separate category for original screenplay for the Oscars, but the task of creating something specifically for the screen is more difficult than adapting something from literature. With adaptation, writers already have a blueprint. There is an economic dimension to consider with adaptation as well: producers are more likely to

embrace an adapted screenplay knowing that audiences already are familiar with it.

Next to the literary traditions discussed in Chapter 2, the major tradition to influence how academics interpreted film was the **psychoanalytical tradition** that remains popular within film studies to this day. One of the first film scholars to adopt a psychoanalytical approach was Parker Tyler, an American writer educated in the same literary traditions as Gilbert Seldes and Robert Warshow. Tyler believed that a Freudian interpretation best suited film because this medium held all the power of myth, magic, and emotion of the collective psyche. Tyler wrote in *Magic and Myth of the Movies* that "movies, similar to much else in life, are seldom what they seem. In this sense— being, to begin with, fiction—movies are dreamlike and fantastic" (Tyler, 1947, p. xii). Films were the manifestation of the dreams, hopes, fears, and anxieties of the directors, actors, and those who rushed to watch them. Films were popular because they tapped into something hidden in our subconscious that projected well onto the screen, and those directors, like Alfred Hitchcock, who understood the psychological connection between the public and films were the most successful in Hollywood.

The psychoanalytical approach to films can explain the popularity of Hitchcock's films. For instance, *Rearview Mirror* captures our voyeuristic desires that are evident today through "reality" television and scandal newspapers. Such an approach can also explain our anxieties. For instance, when millions of men and women are fighting in wars, films often reflect our fears and offer ways to understand how we can overcome our fears. This is why John Wayne was popular in World War II and Sylvester Stallone during the late Cold War period.

The most famous work dealing with a psychoanalytical approach to film is Siegfred Kracauer. Kracauer was part of the Frankfurt School faculty exiled from Germany. In 1947, he completed his famous study of German film, *From Caligari to Hitler: A Psychological History of German Film*. Kracauer believed that post-World War I films captured the anxieties that Germans harbored all through

---

Psychoanalytical Tradition

refers to the theories of the conscious and subconscious states of mind developed by Sigmund Freud and later Jacques Lacan.

the Weimar period. "In recording the visible world," Kracauer believed, "films . . . provide clues to hidden mental processes" (Kracauer, 1947, p. 7). The horror film is one of the genres that best unveil these "hidden mental processes." The Germans were the first to produce horror films, starting a genre that continues with the *Scream* series and the campy "Jason" films. For Kracauer, *The Cabinet of Dr. Caligari* (1920), written by Jans Janowitz and Carl Mayer, was the first of its kind to represent the anxiety and anger Germans had with authority. The German middle class was fearful of revolution but also angered by the abuse of authority that sent millions of young people to their deaths in World War I. Dr. Caligari symbolized these concerns, as did the mechanical robot in *The Golem* or the vampire in *Nosferatu*. Each of these villains manipulated others into committing crimes of murder while the filmmakers often showed that the alternative was chaos and confusion. These anxieties and the inability to act on them were two of the reasons why democratic roots never developed in Weimar Germany and why Hitler was able to gain power in 1933.

Today the principles outlined above still influence how we experience films. The issue of realism is still present in most people's interest in film. Motion has become more of an intense experience since silent films. Sound and the movement of films toward virtual reality (complete immersion of the body and mind of the viewer) through the rise of OmniMax theaters and even traditional theaters with their improved seating and sound systems have made films more effective in convincing the mind that what one sees on the screen and hears all around is right there before the eye. The camera can rush us down a mountainside as our bodies get the same feeling as if we were on roller coaster, or the camera can let us experience the panic of a wildebeest on the Serengeti as it runs for miles away from a dangerous predator.

The one difference between realism in early films and in contemporary films is the blurring between reality and simulation. Early films were not able to effectively blur the lines between the two. *The Matrix* trilogy not only

blurs the lines between real actors and simulations, but it drags viewers into these situations as Laurence Fishburne, Carrie Ann Moss, and Keanu Reeves enter into discussions concerning what is the real world and what is simulation. Contemporary films act as reminders that reality is a simulation and simulation is reality. There is not one area of modern life where the two do not blur. In medicine, simulations are used to detect health risks such as strokes; in economics, simulations create corporate forecasts that guide our stock choices; in sports, we see strategies played out before our eyes through simulated video game formations; and, in relationships, we interact with other people in MUDs (Multi-User Domains) and other simulated situations. The desire for realism is no more intense than it was in early films, but today it is just enhanced more through sound and computer graphics.

The paradox of distance also remains an issue. Moviegoers are still enthralled with entering into a relationship with screen actors. This has changed a little as well. Many moviegoers continue to be interested in Ben and J-Lo or the dress styles and nightlife activities of actors, but many have become interested in the voices of the actors. Some actors are recognized by their voices. For instance, many adults go to animated films to hear who is lending his or her voice to which character. This desire to know the voices of characters is connected to the interest in closing the distance between the actors and moviegoers. When we hear their voices we enter into the film and into a relationship with the character-actors who are obviously not present for every viewing of the film, while we are not present when they give a voice to an animated character in *Shrek, Finding Nemo, The Simpsons,* or *Rugrats.* Overcoming the paradox of distance is one way for moviegoers, and later we will see for television-watchers as well, to break free of the limitations of their material lives and experience life in ways they normally would not be able to. This is a power we should not pathologize but embrace in all facets of our lives.

Finally, the immortality principle is still prevalent today. This principle has changed, too, with the advent of

virtual reality and surround sound. Now moviegoers can have a complete experience of overcoming the limitations of time. The screen is no longer a prison house but, as Robin Williams' movie *What Dreams May Come* shows, heaven is what you make and remake it to be. In films, virtual reality has permitted us to create numerous possibilities that best suit our desires. With the growing prominence of DVDs, films now present multiple endings and with the premiere of *Twenty-Eight Days* and its re-release 28 days later with a new ending, film viewers see the possibilities of playing with reality and warding off the realities of time. This desire to cheat death, as Bazin wrote about 50 years ago, no matter how fleeting or momentary the effect may be, is still a prominent aspect of film.

Television

The issue of distance is also present in television. The first person to think about the impact of television was Marshall McLuhan. He believed that television "affected the totality of our lives." The viewer was drawn into the screen, making television an "extremely intimate" experience (McLuhan, 1964/1994, p. 317). While the filmgoer entered into a relationship with the camera, the viewer related to the television screen. For McLuhan, the television screen, like all new electronic devices, altered our central nervous systems. "Cool" (see Chapter 2) in intensity and data resolution, McLuhan still believed television greatly changed how we interacted with the world, changing how our nervous systems were "wired" to interpret our surroundings.

While the screen altered our nervous system, other scholars such as Samuel Weber interpreted the screen's impact on our lives differently. Television "serves as a screen which allows distant vision to be watched." Given this ability to shrink distances, television, or "seeing from a distance" is an appropriate name for this technological device. Television's importance is further enhanced because "it screens, in the sense of selecting or filtering, the vision that is watched. And finally, it serves as a screen in

the sense of standing between the viewer and the viewed" (Weber, 1996, p. 122–123). Of these three meanings for television as a screen, it is the second that is the most powerful and important to highlight. As a filter, television not only brings distant objects to us so we can see the world from our living room, but it also decides what we can see of the world. Television shapes the world because it selects what parts of the world we will see. This ability to shape what others see is nothing less than a power that should be only in the hands of the "public." It is also because of this ability to be selective that debates about democracy and communication systems are common when talking about the impact of television on society.

Television as a democratic filter is Raymond Williams' interest in the medium. For Williams, television solved two important problems modernity created: alienation and mobility. Television brought the world to the modern individual who was feeling more isolated in industrial society. While people might not see their neighbors often or have much time to go out in public, television served as a conduit for socialization. On any given night, people could be entertained by Bob Hope, Lucille Ball, Jackie Gleason, Monty Python, *The Eastenders*, and all of their movie favorites.

Television also helped overcome the problems caused by mobility. Capitalism uprooted people. While people were able to find low-paying work in the city, they had to move from the communities they grew up in. Television offered a new public domain that could reconnect people to some form of culture. Williams believed that if television were to overcome alienation and mobility, it had to serve the public and remain in the public's control. As a result, the importance of television was not what programs it offered, but rather who controlled its flow. From its inception, Williams argued against the dominance of commercial television. Corporations served their own interests and could not be trusted with the public's airwaves. Of course, today Williams' concerns have fallen on mostly deaf ears. The airwaves are considered public but commercialization has controlled television for decades. One can

even argue that airwaves are owned only in name by the public since most people have to pay a cable company to receive even the basic channels.

Another scholar concerned with democracy and television is Jacques Derrida. Like Williams, Derrida wants to create an active viewer and to do so people have to be involved in all dimensions of television. "What is possible and, in my opinion, desirable," Derrida states, "are not legislative decisions concerning the production and distribution of whatever it is, but open programs of education and training in the use of this technology, these technical means. You would have to do everything possible so that, citizens or not, the users of the technical instruments might themselves participate in the production and selection of the programs in question" (Derrida and Steigler, 2002, p. 54). Most television corporations would argue that the people are actively involved via the choices they make and the **Nielsen ratings** that chart these program choices. This, however, is very much a part of the cynicism that Gilbert Seldes warned about in the late 1940s. People are not active participants in television when they are reduced to Nielsen rating points and only permitted to choose from a list of programs created by someone else. Derrida argues that all people should be active participants in creating television, from creating their own programming ideas with their VCRs to creating their own Web pages to facilitate dialogue about television from its function in a democracy to the latest episode of *The Simpsons*.

Douglas Kellner is yet another scholar who is interested in public access to television. Williams and Derrida envision television as a filter with democratic possibilities; Kellner views television as an extension of a capitalist society in which institutions such as television serve the interests of business. As a result, television's logic is one of "accumulation" that "dictates a logic of exclusion that condemns to silence those voices whose criticisms of the capitalist mode of production go beyond the boundaries allowed by the lords of the media" (Kellner, 1990, p. 9). Influenced by the Frankfurt School (see Chapter 2),

Nielsen Ratings
still the main approach television researchers use to determine what people are watching.

Kellner offers an alternative to corporate television. Instead of paying "lip service" to democratic principles, Kellner suggests that accountability, access, and adequacy (whether programming serves public interests) are required principles to establish television as a public domain. Of these principles, access and adequacy are keystones to Kellner's ideas. Access implies the same thing that Derrida envisioned. If television were accessible, the public would be involved in all facets of television production, from programming to advertising. One way to ensure access is adequacy. In order to know if the programming available is meeting the needs of people, one has to enter into a dialogue or debate not only over what the public wants but what the public is. Kellner suggests that to ensure adequacy of programming, there must be public access channels, more support for public television stations, and ongoing debates over what issues should be addressed by television programs. Debates over the adequacy of television will foster a democratic ethos rather than an ethos in which corporate profits and consumption are privileged over the rights of individuals.

John Fiske offers a different approach to television than those presented above. Although he is interested in issues of democracy, Fiske is interested in how people "read" television. Using a semiotic approach, or how people construct meaning from television, Fiske believes that television, like all cultural forms, contains codes. These "codes are links between producers, texts, and audiences, and are the agents of intertexuality through which texts interrelate in a network of meanings" (Fiske, 1987, p. 4). Once television is interpreted as a conveyer of cultural codes and these codes are read, television is transformed from something that is produced to something that is textual. As a text, the meaning of television becomes **polysemic** or multiple. The important issue for Fiske, therefore, is not the meanings that television corporations wish to portray in their programming but how people read television. When television is transformed into a text, instability and uncertainty enters the picture and a struggle over meaning ensues. Which meaning prevails with viewers

Polysemic

refers to words and images as seeds. When spoken or viewed, they spread and grow wherever they are planted.

Discourse
a language system that represents the world and circulates throughout society to create a culture within the world.

depends on which **discourse** viewers adopt to construct the television program they are "reading."

What follows are two examples of how television shows are polysemic and are read in different ways: *Roseanne* and *The Waltons*. When this chapter discusses fan cultures later, it will also show how television series are read in interesting ways.

When *Roseanne* first appeared on television in 1987, it was greeted with boisterous criticism because Roseanne Barr, later Roseanne Arnold and then just Roseanne, was not the stereotypical television mother. Read from this angle, *Roseanne* was iconoclastic and not the kind of television "good" parents would want their children to watch. However, read from a different angle, *Roseanne* could be read as the most realistic television show ever produced. Roseanne and the other creators of the show were always mindful of the construction of motherhood and family life on television. The mother always stayed at home while the father worked and the children, while sometimes rebellious, always did the right thing. There were no problems that could not be solved in 22 minutes with a few commercials in between. In *Roseanne*'s Conner family, problems were real. Unemployment always was a threat to their lifestyle. During one season the father, Dan Conner, played by John Goodman, risked the family savings to open up a motorcycle shop. The shop went bankrupt and as a result the oldest daughter's college fund was lost. On *Roseanne*, dreams were risked and lost just as they are in real life. It can be argued that *Roseanne* was the first realistic television show that represented the uncertainties of life.

Another example is *The Waltons*. Read from the lens of today's world of cellphones, Hummers, and yuppie superficiality, the Waltons are outdated. They can also be read as the embodiment of conservative family values in which the dignity and sanctity of life always prospered over the "choices" of individuals. However, read from a different angle, *The Waltons* can be read as an outlet for progressive causes. As Fiske notes, the codes of a television program manifest themselves in three ways: in the reality of the show (appearance, environment, speech), in the representation of the show (lights, camera angles, editing), and in the ideology (race, class, gender, economic, and political issues). It is in the last code that one can see the progressive potential of *The Waltons*. In the television show, Olivia Walton is a no-nonsense, Baptist, stay at-home mother, but during the credits the actor is introduced as Miss Michael Learned. When this first appeared in 1972 these credits were controversial, but Learned insisted that this is how she should be introduced—as an independent woman. Progressivism manifested itself in other ways as well. The grandfather was played by Will Geer. Geer was a blacklisted actor who stood up to right-wing bullies in the 1950s and fought for people's dignity in the 1930s as a folksinger with Woody Guthrie. During his seven seasons on the show before he died in 1978, Geer offered well-written soliloquies about being the caretakers of the environment and of each other. The father, played by Ralph Waite, held similar views. Waite ran unsuccessfully as a progressive candidate for Congress in the 1980s and 1990s, and as an actor he used his role as John Walton to stress the need to not judge people based on their race, gender, creed, or sexual orientation.

These two examples and the work of John Fiske demonstrate that television is an open book. The authors of this open book may have their own intentions, but the reader has the ultimate freedom to interpret them in ways producers and corporate sponsors may not sanction. If television cannot offer this much, it would not be a medium worth the space it takes up in the home.

Music

In its song "PWEI vs. the Moral Majority," the British, techno-band Pop Will Eat Itself opens with a minister's sermon in which the pastor cites Plato, Aristotle, and Lenin. He proclaims that each of these thinkers believes that if one wants to change society one has to change music. The minister is correct. Music has played an instrumental role in society since the human species first began.

Plato, for instance, believed that music was a primary way to educate the young in understanding the harmony of the universe and their station in it.

The most prolific scholar of music and culture is Theodore Adorno. Platonic in his beliefs that music had an essence that could not be captured in words, Adorno believed music in the 20th century was in crisis. The crisis took many shapes including the commercialization and commodification of music, the leveling or classification of music, the reduced role of the artist in musical production, and the dominance of technology in the dissemination of music. For Adorno the labeling of music as "classical," "jazz," or "dance" reduced all music to classifications and prevented listeners from distinguishing between great music (e.g., Mahler and Schoenberg) and bourgeois music (e.g., jazz). The biggest threat to music was technology. The gramophone and phonograph separated the voice from the body, destroying any subjective connections one might create between themselves, the music, and the artist. The only good Adorno found in technology was that "the dead art rescues the ephemeral and perishing art as the only one alive. Therein may lie the phonograph record's most profound justification" (Adorno, 2002, p. 279). The phonograph as a dead art preserves the art of music as the photograph or film were seen as preserving a life.

Adorno saved his most critical comments for jazz. If technology and commodification were threatening music, jazz was the embodiment of these threats. Jazz captured the superficiality of bourgeois societies and "is not a generative force, but a recourse to false origins under the control of destruction" (Adorno, 2002, p. 477). If jazz contained any hope for the development of music, it was lost after its early popularity in the United States. Jazz was reduced to military marches and salon music, where trendy and superficial people met to demonstrate their lack of substance. Jazz, more than any other form of culture, proved to Adorno that mass culture was not healthy.

Music criticism since Adorno has been more open to popular culture. If jazz represented the most popular

Hip-hop
the broad term that encompasses the musical forms of rap, break dancing, graffiti art, language formations, and fashions originally associated with African Americans from the urban centers of the United States.

music during Adorno's early career from the 1930s to the 1940s, then it is not an overstatement to suggest that **hip-hop** is the most popular music today. The difference is that most music critics are open to the power of hip-hop. Tricia Rose was one of the first scholars to write about the phenomenon of hip-hop and is correct in locating its rise within the context of de-industrialization and white flight from urban centers in the United States. Hip-hop is characterized by its "hybridity," or the ability to take from its environment and capture the sounds and feelings of the world around it. When hip-hop's musical style, rap, emerged in 1979 it was dismissed as a fad that would fade. Today, hip-hop is a multi-billion-dollar industry that transcends all racial, national, ethnic, religious, gender, and sexual barriers.

Imani Perry refers to hip-hop artists as the freelance intellectuals of the de-industrializing world. The style and message of these artists often is reduced to the "gangsta" rap of Dr. Dre, Snoop Dog, or Tupac, but such a reduction blunts the depth and meaning of hip-hop. There is not one group, except perhaps stiff-necked, white middle-class adults, who are not represented by some group in hip-hop. William Perkins points out that Islamic rap is on the rise and "Islamic rappers bring to hip-hop a powerful sense of recovering and reinventing history, packaging it as 'science' for the visual generation" (Perkins, 1996, p. 23). There are also German, French, Pacific Islander, Japanese, and Korean hip-hop movements.

What makes hip-hop an interesting cultural phenomenon is the exact thing that Adorno criticized as the death blow of modern music: technology. Hip-hop artists co-opt

Iteration
a termed borrowed from literary criticism to describe the ability to construct one context from another without the words losing their old meaning while new meanings are created.

in a cultural moment of **iteration**, adapting items such as old vinyl albums, turntables, street corners, and amplifiers to create their music. Hip-hop's ability to adopt numerous forms of technology creates an outlet for many youth who have expressed a "widespread disaffection from the machinery of capitalism at a time when the free market is widely hailed in the media as the great economic savior" (Potter, 1995, p. 10).

From Spectators to Fan Cultures

When Germany was unified in 1871, the new chancellor, Otto von Bismarck, observed that "now that we have Germany we have to invent Germans." The same can be true about spectators and film. When the new medium of film emerged, filmgoers had to be invented. Early movie producers and theater companies taught people how to watch a film. Before films, people were accustomed to live performances on stage or vaudeville performances. If the performance was offensive, audience members were not averse to throwing things at the performers; likewise, if the performance was stellar, audience members sometimes would join the cast members on stage at the end of the show. When films were first shown, however, this type of behavior could not be tolerated. Anyone who threw objects at the screen would damage it and anyone who tried to join the film stars on stage would simply look foolish interacting with a projected image. Moviegoers also had to get used to the open format of film viewing. In the early days of filmmaking, directors and producers would shoot their films, sometimes edit them, and then ship the reels off to movie houses. Which reel was shown first was up to the movie-house manager. Movie houses also employed "lecturers" who created a narrative so people could have a sense of what the plot was in the film. These dimensions of early filmmaking created an open atmosphere for spectators to view films. As directors perfected the art of editing and defined which reels of film should be viewed first, the interpretive possibilities of the spectator became limited. By 1916, spectators were expected to be passive receptors of a narrative that was already pre-packaged by the movie company. Within a short time frame of 20 years in early film viewing a certain protocol emerged that expected people to remain in their seats, avoid talking and any other disruptions, and literally "sit back and relax" while they were entertained.

Since the protocol of early spectatorship, fan cultures in television, films, and music have changed dramatically. While early spectators were expected to be passive, fans

have since found ways to interact with their favorite media. The seminal work in understanding fan cultures is Henry Jenkins' *Textual Poachers: Television Fans & Participatory Culture.*

Jenkins adopts Michel de Certeau's idea of textual poaching to explain how people interact with television programs. For de Certeau, poaching is a form of active reading in which the reader establishes his or her own meaning of the text. Textual poachers, de Certeau claimed, took from the text only what they found to be useful and pleasurable and read the text according to those standards rather than the standards of culture, tastes, or authorial intent. Those who tried to impose meaning on the readers de Certeau called "scriptural readers." They were the vanguard or border police who tried to sanction meaning and dictate what one should feel when engaged in the act of reading.

Jenkins took this concept and applied it to television fans. As poachers, television watchers selected their favorite television shows, created common bonds with other viewers, formed clubs, and established chat lines in order to discuss various dimensions of the television show, from plot and character developments to fantasies that were often homoerotic. Jenkins writes about various shows, including *Star Trek, Star Trek: The Next Generation, Alien Nation, Twin Peaks,* and *Beauty and the Beast.* It is his work on *Beauty and the Beast* that best highlights the interaction of television poachers and scriptural readers.

Beauty and the Beast was a CBS series that lasted only two and a half years, but which generated a large and loyal fan base. Fans communicated with each other via local club gatherings and Internet chat lines. During this time, fans rewrote scripts, extended the interactions of characters, and speculated on the romantic relationships between Linda Hamilton's character and the beast, played by Ron Pearlman. After the second season, network executives decided to end the series. The loyal fans revolted by writing letters to *TV Guide* and petitioning CBS. Eventually the network relented and decided to run the series for at least one more year. However, the fans were

discouraged that Linda Hamilton decided not to come back and CBS decided to kill off her character as a result. Fans were unhappy with the producers' decisions and the writing of the third season and as a result the show's ratings plummeted. The show was canceled without a full third-year run.

Jenkins' work demonstrates how people, in spite of scriptural vanguards, interact with television as texts whose meanings are open to numerous interpretations. He also chronicles how *Star Trek* fans over the years created a subculture of meaning through fan clubs, **fanzines**, and **slash writers**. What Jenkins demonstrates in his study is that fan cultures are as dynamic and creative as any other cultural form that has ever manifested itself in modern societies.

Another example of how individuals interact with popular culture is John Fiske's work *Power Play, Power Works*. Fiske provides numerous examples, including how Elvis fans interact with impersonators and how unauthorized DJs "highjack" the airwaves to broadcast their message. Another group he focuses on is a group of Midwestern homeless men who interacted with film, especially Bruce Willis' *Die Hard*. Fiske notes that the men cheered when the "villain," played by Alan Rickman of *Harry Potter* fame, executes the CEO of the fictitious Nakatomi Corporation, but before Bruce Willis can restore order and reinstate the leaders of capitalism in their halls of power, the homeless men turned the VCR off. Fiske suggests that the power to read the film as an uprooting of capitalist order that lead to the homelessness of the men is a **localizing power,** while the power of the movie companies and leaders of the capitalist order is an **imperializing power**. Although their power is very limited, Fiske tries to demonstrate how as fans of movies these homeless men construct their own meaning of the film. This ability to construct meaning provides them with a little power to control their local surroundings. In the world of imperializing power where wealth and influence are in the concentrated hands of a few people, sometimes the only power most people possess is the ability to interpret enter-

Fanzines

magazines created by fans.

Slash Writers

mostly females who take *Star Trek* episodes, usually those dealing with Spock and Kirk, and place them in homoerotic situations to express subplots that could never be expressed on the television show.

Localizing Power

nothing more than the ability to control one's local surroundings.

Imperializing Power

a much more pervasive power that tries to extend its reach simply because it can.

tainment in ways that they find useful and pleasurable, as fans. Although imperializing powers try to manipulate people's thoughts, Fiske demonstrates that the creative area of the mind is the last place people can control.

A final example of fan cultures is Daniel Cavicchi's work on Springsteen fans. Cavicchi offers a detailed ethnographical approach to music cultures. He focuses on Springsteen fans because since he was eight years old in 1975 and Springsteen released *Born to Run* Cavicchi himself has been a fan. Being both a fan and an academic creates a problem for him because, as Cavicchi points out, academics have labeled fans as "fanatics," "unstable," "irrational," and "groupies." Fans are very much aware of these stigmas. Cavicchi found that while researching Springsteen fans, they were suspicious whether Cavicchi was a "true" fan and if he was really interested in what they thought. What is most illuminating about Cavicchi's work is he demonstrates that fans are searching for answers and often find them in the companionship of fellow fans and in the lyrics of their favorite musicians. In a gripping and telling passage, Cavicchi demonstrates the impact of fan culture on his own life. He notes: "I have found that my fandom for various musical performers has . . . gotten me through many tough times over the years and has been the source of many friendships, including my relationship with my wife" (Cavicchi, 1998, p. 8). It is statements like this that demonstrate the importance of understanding fan cultures and the failure of traditional cultural institutions such as the family and churches to deal with the needs of people.

Glossary

Expressionism is a 20th-century art movement based on the distortion of images and color. Filmmakers utilized expressionism in Germany to highlight the theme of most of their movies: the uncertainty and chaos of modernity brought about by authoritarian leaders who convinced people to commit barbaric acts.

Montage is a style adopted from photography and painting that places more than one image into a frame to signal to the filmgoer the multiple parts that make up the whole film.

Psychoanalytical Tradition refers to the theories of the conscious and subconscious states of mind developed by Sigmund Freud and later Jacques Lacan.

Nielsen Ratings are still the main approach that television researchers use to determine what people are watching. Historically, the ratings are statistically flawed and unreliable but television executives found that when they approached companies to sell advertising slots, the companies were more likely to pay higher prices for slots if the television stations had some statistics to demonstrate how many people were watching television during a certain time slot.

Polysemic refers to words and images as seeds. When spoken or viewed, they spread and grow wherever they are planted. How they grow and develop depends on each individual and how these individuals interpret the words and images.

Discourse is a language system that represents the world and circulates throughout society to create a culture within the world.

Hip-hop is the broad term that encompasses the musical forms of rap, break dancing, graffiti art, language formations, and fashions originally associated with African Americans from the urban centers of the United States. Now hip-hop is a global phenomenon that influences youth throughout the world.

Iteration is a termed borrowed from literary criticism to describe the ability to construct one context from another without the words losing their old meaning while new meanings are created. J. Hillis Miller explains the meaning of iteration and its power best: "Iterability is nothing more . . . than the possibility for every mark to be repeated and still to function as a meaningful mark in new contexts that are cut off entirely from the original context, the 'intention' to communicate' of the original maker of the mark" (Miller, 2001, p. 78). There is no doubt hip-hop artists are some of the best practitioners of iteration.

Fanzines are magazines created by fans. These magazines, however, are not to be sold for a profit but are written only for those people who wish to discuss and understand the inner details of a television show.

Slash Writers are mostly females who take *Star Trek* episodes, usually those dealing with Spock and Kirk, and place them in homoerotic situations to express subplots that could never be expressed on the television show. Constance Penley notes that slash writing is a way for women to interject their

thoughts into the creative process, especially on a show that often limits the roles of women to sex kittens in short skirts.

Localizing Power is nothing more than the ability to control one's local surroundings.

Imperializing Power is a much more pervasive power that tries to extend its reach simply because it can.

CHAPTER FOUR

The Cultural Studies of Technoscience

There are two points to address at the beginning of this chapter. The first is that most books dealing with popular culture, whether introductory or not, usually ignore the **cultural studies of technoscience**. Yet many of the most dynamic and interesting theories are coming from people who would associate themselves in some way with the cultural studies of science. The other point to make centers around the term "technoscience." Traditionally, scholars of science, such as Richard Merton and Joseph Ben-David, insisted that science (i.e., pure, basic) and technology (i.e., applied, engineering) were separate entities with the former intellectually superior to the latter. Such a position cannot hold under the strain of reality. Corporations are running university laboratories; computer companies and professors are creating joint venture start-up companies; and the flow of funds move directly among federal agencies, corporations, foundations, and intellectuals. The term "technoscience" marks this shift in the relationship between scientists and the things they create. This chapter will cover some traditions of under-

Cultural Studies of Technoscience
a generic term that includes scholars who are interested in the history, philosophy, sociology, anthropology, and rhetoric of science.

standing the role of science and technology in our society, the rise of interdisciplinary approaches to the cultural
studies of science, the emergence of the posthuman condition and other techno-cultures, and the so-called "science wars."

Traditions of Science Studies

Before the 1960s, it was common folklore within the
science fields to characterize science as an intellectual
endeavor that was objective (free of interpretive frame-
works), or as the anthropologist of science Sharon Traweek
suggests "the culture of no culture." It was considered
devoted to realism (what took place in the laboratory or any
site of scientific work corresponded with the reality of
nature), disinterested (politics was not a part of science and
scientists were not interested in making value judgments
about the world or nature; they were just interested in the
facts), autonomous (scientists who did basic or pure science were free of economic constraints such as government and corporate connections), and truth-based rather
than ideological (science was not ideological). By 1945,
such a perspective could not hold much of a grip on reality, if it ever had a serious grip at all. First, from this ethos
of science grew a paradox. If scientists were not "of this
world" and were autonomous amd free from worldly
demands, how could they speak to the conditions of the
world? Or how could someone disconnected from nature
come to know anything directly from nature? Second,
each one of these conditions mentioned above has been
compromised by concrete circumstances in science. If
science is objective, how does one get a fact to speak?
Can a fact speak for itself? And if not, then who will speak
for it and in what language and style? If someone speaks
for a fact of nature, is it not reasonable to assume that the
codes, values, and beliefs of the speaker influence in some
way how those facts are represented? This takes us to the
next issue, realism. If facts cannot speak for themselves,
then how are facts represented? How do electron micro-
scopes, weather monitoring devices, supercolliders, and

other scientific machines shape what we see and represent what we know? Can we directly know the world without some intervening device? Can scientists be disinterested and autonomous when they are receiving funds from the federal government, for instance, creating nerve gas for the war effort as German, English, French, and American chemists did in World War I? Can biochemists be disinterested when their work will be used in the creation of the next pharmaceutical wonder drug? And if history tells us that none of these principles can hold any weight under scrutiny, then does that make all scientists ideologues who have abandoned the search for truth? Of course not, but it places in doubt any neat dichotomies that claim to distinguish between truth and ideology. Traditional approaches came under attack by the 1960s, and scholars interested in science studies sought to develop new theories about how science works.

Thomas Kuhn and Paradigm Shifts

Thomas Kuhn was studying to be a physicist when he became interested in the history of science. In his book *The Structure of Scientific Revolutions*, Kuhn suggested that science is not the accumulation of facts and progression toward the truth. Science is more like a competition between various theories that are **incommensurable** with one another. As to which theory comes to dominate the others, Kuhn suggested there is a cycle to determine this. First, there is normal science. This constitutes the idea that there is an acceptable paradigm (theory of thought accepted as the protocol for doing research and thinking about nature) and this paradigm shapes the questions that scientists pursue in their laboratory. This paradigm shapes how people conduct their research, how they think about their research, how research journals are written and reviewed, how grants and other funds are distributed, and how scientists conduct themselves within the confines of scientific endeavors. The dominant paradigm is accepted as such because it continues to produce knowledge and explanations for events in the natural world. Once in a while

Incommensurability
a term Kuhn introduced to suggest that scientific theories represent different cultures, values, beliefs, and laboratory techniques that cannot be compared to each other because of these differences.

anomalies occur, which is the second part of Kuhn's cycle. At first, these anomalies are discarded and dismissed as outliers that can be explained away as exceptions to the rule or accidents caused by careless scientists in the laboratory. However, at pivotal moments in science these anomalies become too powerful to dismiss and a crisis occurs, which is the third part of the cycle. These crises have occurred, for instance, when Copernicus demonstrated that the earth is not the center of our solar system or when Max Planck uncovered the world of quanta and placed Newtonian science in doubt when dealing with the microscopic world. Crises eventually lead to the adoption of a new worldview, the fourth step in Kuhn's cycle. This new worldview leads to a different vision that presents nature in whole new perspective. As a result of the new paradigm, old questions can be asked differently and new questions arise, creating new fields and new research agendas for scientists. Although this cycle might appear as a neat and tidy explanation of scientific work, the consequences for creating new paradigms are serious. It was Galileo who suggested that light bends. However, this went against the accepted paradigm and as a result Galileo was excommunicated from the church and kept under house arrest. It was not until Albert Einstein developed his general theory of relativity that Galileo was proven correct, almost 400 years after his proclamations. As paradigms rise and fall, scientists risk their reputations arguing for one paradigm over another and the politics can be severe.

Although later in his life Kuhn suggested that he did not intend to start his own paradigm shift, he did. As evidence of how important his ideas were, when *The New York Times* created their list of the top 100 influential books of the 20th century, Kuhn's book was the only academic book on the list. Kuhn's ideas opened the door for other people to interpret the work of scientists in nontraditional ways.

Paul Feyerabend was one of those people. In 1975, Feyerabend published *Against Method*. The premise of his book is that if the world were solely dependent on the scientific method to advance our knowledge of the world, we would still be in the Stone Age. Science does not follow a path of careful deliberation and experimentation, considering all possible explanations for a natural phenomenon. Science advances because of expediency, accidents, intuition, and hunches. To prove his point, Feyerabend focuses on Galileo. With the use of his telescopes, Galileo submitted his theory that stars were not in the sky where the naked eye told us they were. Light bends, he said, and when we look into the sky at the stars, the curvature of the light distorts our vision. The telescope compensates for this distortion and shows the actual positions of the stars. At the time, Galileo had no mathematical proof to support his claim, only his intuition and hunch. When he tried to defend his position against the Roman Catholic Church and its scientists, he asked them to look into his telescope to prove his point. The church scientists saw what they were trained to see, concluded that looking at stars in a telescope did not prove anything, and dismissed Galileo's theory as heresy against accepted scientific facts.

Cosmic Webs and Science Studies

Another person who took advantage of Kuhn's open door is N. Katherine Hayles. Hayles suggests that within the realm of intellectual history there are core ideas that capture the attention of scholars during the same time period—scholars who are not familiar with each other's work. Hayles refers to this phenomenon as a cosmic web. A web has different paths woven throughout its pattern; one can follow a single path and never reach another part of the web, but it is still a part of the web: they are still interconnected. To prove her point, in each of her books Hayles takes examples from science (field theory, chaos theory, and information science), theory (deconstruction, feminism, and postmodernism), and literature. Hayles notes, for instance, that while scientists and mathematicians such as Ilya Prigogine and Benoit Mandelbrot were creating theories dealing with self-organization and fractals, Jacques Derrida, Doris Lessing, Stanislaw Lem, and Jean Francois Lyotard were doing the same thing in literature and phi-

losophy. When Claude Shannon, John Von Neumann, and Norbert Wiener were devising mathematical theories about information flows and cybernetics, Philip K. Dick and Neal Stephenson were doing the same thing in literature. Hayles does not suggest that one field of study gets its inspiration from another field, but she does suggest that similar ideas are adopted roughly at the same time and that each individual creates his or her own path from the cosmic web of ideas.

Machines and Science Studies

It should not surprise anyone that once a paradigm shift is started the individual or group that began the process has regrets or does not sanction every approach that emerges from the new paradigm. Therefore, Kuhn's displeasure with some of the paths taken in his name is not a surprise. One thing Kuhn did not speak much about is how paradigms often contain the seeds of their demise. Kuhn's theory of paradigm shifts is no exception. Peter Galison and numerous other scholars have begun to discuss the limits of Kuhn's theories. First, they note that perhaps Kuhn's paradigm is not as much of a shift as originally thought. Kuhn remains a traditionalist in that he continues the pattern within science of privileging pure or basic science over technology and the notion that theory is superior to application. Second, the notion of a paradigm shift focuses its attention on mental or intellectual shifts while ignoring other dimensions that cause science to change. In his book *Image and Logic*, Galison is interested in "the history of instruments" (Galison, 1997, p. 51). Instruments and the laboratories that they call home have a life that extends beyond their role in science. It is not only through individuals that economics, politics, and culture enter into science but instruments and laboratories as well. If one looks at the ways in which instruments are developed and used, one can see how theories have developed around these usages. Moreover, if one looks at the development of laboratories, one can see how science shifts from one based on individual "bench work" to one in

which federal agencies, organizational management, and grant writing are involved. Things may not speak, but if one studies the interaction of things with humans, instruments and laboratories tell an interesting story.

In a good example of the "cosmic web" working, Timothy Lenoir published his major work *Instituting Science: The Cultural Production of Scientific Disciplines* the same year that Galison's work appeared. Lenoir joins Galison (or is it Galison joining Lenoir?) to move beyond the realm of paradigms and ideas and into the realm of everyday life in science. While Galison focuses on instruments, Lenoir's concentration is on institutions. He is interested in how science is disciplined as a field and as a result how these disciplines (chemistry, physics, biology, and later biochemistry) permit and limit what scientists can think and do. As Lenoir notes, "Institutions guide, enable, and constrain nearly every aspect of our lives" (Lenoir, 1997, p. 1). Every scientific field, as is the case for every laboratory, contains its own culture, and those people who come to represent and embody that culture are the ones who are able to garner as much freedom as possible to conduct their research and construct their theories. As for those people who are "deficient in the requisite culture, lacking both explicit and tacit knowledge of how the institution works, [they] run spang into concrete walls" (Lenoir, 1997, p. 2). These walls can take the form of denied funding for a project, papers rejected by conferences, publications rejected by peer reviewers, and denied tenure. Like most other cultures, the cultures of science can be, and often are, cruel and unusual in their punishment for those who are unaware of the inner workings of institutions.

Actor Network Theory

Actor network theory is yet another approach that emerged after Kuhn's theory of paradigm shifts. The theory is that to learn more about scientists' work, one should follow them around. This is Bruno Latour's mantra, which explains the subtitle of his most famous work, *Science in Action: How to Follow Scientists and Engineers through Society.* Latour's subtitle is a quirky and voyeuristic way of

saying he is advocating an ethnographical approach to science studies. In *Science in Action*, Latour takes three scenes from the history of science and charts how these moments moved from disorderly phenomena in nature to earning places in the order of things, called scientific facts.

One of the dimensions in this journey of scientific fact construction that Latour focuses on is the role of scientific journals. Latour suggests that there are three steps that begin the process of constructing scientific facts through article writing. 1) "Bringing friends in": This steps requires the writer to connect with allies within the field of study who already have established their niche or regime of facts within the field. This constructs a journal article through what Latour refers to as "argument from authority" (Latour, 1987, p. 31). 2) "Referring to former texts": This is an issue of piling on, of showing that the evidence overwhelmingly supports the premise of the article. It is an issue of numbers: the more you cite, the more persuasive the article will be perceived to be. 3) "Being referred to by later texts": This begins the process of layering, in which one's article becomes a part of a research regime and a paradigm in which one's article is cited as proof that other articles are truth-telling documents. Once one's article is in this loop of citations, the stakes rise to a new level. If for some reason one's article is later challenged and proven to be false or inaccurate, such a challenge causes a chain reaction in which the article challenged is not the only document placed in doubt. Every article that cited it as a statement of scientific fact is also placed in doubt.

One should not adopt the posture that the struggle to construct a scientific fact through journals is about name-dropping, piling on, and citations indexes. These strategies, Latour notes, are constantly challenged throughout the life of a journal article. What interests Latour and the actor network theory of science is not necessarily how a scientist's claims are proven ultimately to be correct or not but rather how these claims circulate throughout the scientific communities.

The major point to glean from an actor network theory is that scholars such as Latour, Steven Woolgar, Karin

Knorr Cetina, and Harry Collins do not limit their ethnographical wonderings to people. They also include nonhumans. To understand the life of a scientist and the cultures of laboratory science, one has to listen to machines and understand how things shape the culture of science. Science is truly a posthuman endeavor, as humans, machines, animals, and nature converge within this culture and constructed meaning about the nature of machines, humans, and animals are hammered out daily and then reshaped in new ways the next day.

Interdisciplinary Science: The Materiality of Culture

One of the more interesting developments within the cultural studies of science is the impressive interdisciplinary approach scholars adopt within the field. Most of the scholars mentioned in this section and the next dealing with the posthuman condition are included for two reasons: these scholars hail mainly from literature programs and all remind their readers of the importance of the materiality of culture.

Although these scholars are associated with literature programs, most have graduate training in the sciences. This interdisciplinary dimension of their careers can be explained in two ways. First, since the appearance of C.P. Snow's monograph on *The Two Cultures* (humanities and sciences) there has been an attempt to end the antagonism between the two cultures. Humanists proclaim that scientists do not have a true function within the traditional university and are too practical and technical in their worldview. Scientists have complained that humanists are too elitist and dogmatic in their understanding of what knowledge is and what the purpose of the university is. Scholars from literature in the last 20 years, including William Paulson, have tried to bridge this gap between the two cultures. Paulson suggests that universities need to construct a third culture in which the university facilitates interdisciplinary projects between the so-called two cultures so that each group can see the valuable insights of the other. To date, the project has been quite success-

ful. Katherine Hayles has combined her graduate degrees in chemistry and literature to construct insightful works; Donna Haraway has combined biology with cultural criticism to provide the most enlightening commentary on the cultural impact of science; Arkady Plotnitsky has utilized his advanced degrees in mathematics and comparative literature to demonstrate the similarities between ideas in philosophy, literature, and science; and Mark Hansen has benefited from his interdisciplinary studies to comment on philosophy and digital cultures.

There is a second reason why literary scholars have ventured into interdisciplinary work, a reason more serious than the first. Literature as a discipline and a viable department in most universities is in serious decline. As a result, literary scholars are looking for new areas to explore, and science and cultural studies have proven to be two of the more fruitful areas to date. The reasons for this decline are numerous. One can begin with the transformation of the university from and environment that nurtures culture and citizens for the nation-state to one that is **performative**.

Performative and Instrumental terms that refer to the belief that knowledge is not good in and of itself but must enter into an exchange market in which knowledge as information can be exchanged for more valuable goods and services.

Jean Francois Lyotard, in his work *The Postmodern Condition*, was one of the first people to chart this shift in the university's mission in the 1970s. Literature in the traditional university was a main way to create citizens of a nation-state. One person was considered English because he or she could cite Shakespeare, and another was considered American because he or she read Melville, Hawthorne, and Thoreau. With the rise of the performative or **instrumental** university, literature is important only if it can get a student a job and it is only palatable as a discipline if its knowledge can be reduced to commodified information that can be later exchanged for a degree and money.

Literature as a discipline is also declining because of economic and population shifts that transcend national boundaries. With the nation-state no longer the standard bearer of identity, multinational corporations and nomadic capitalism now serve as the major ways in which identities are formed. Multinational corporations transcend national boundaries and supersede the laws of nations via international trade agreements such as NAFTA and GATT, and different peoples nomadically move from peripherally economic areas to areas of prosperity. These shifts in populations create identity crises for nations such as the United States and England and for universities and literature departments. For instance, traditional literature departments do not make sense when one realizes that the works Shakespeare, Wordsworth, Austin, and Wilde alone do not represent the population of England. These literary giants represent only a portion of the current British population. What is it, then, that makes English literature *literature?* Is it Shakespeare? What about Mark Twain? Is it J.M. Coetzee, who is English but from South Africa? Is it James Baldwin, who is American but spent much of his productive life as an exile in Paris? Or is it C.L.R. James, who is Caribbean? This identity crisis has led many literature departments to rethink themselves within the context of a new university and a new world order. As a result, literary scholars have sought out new rationales for their existence and the cultural studies of science has become one of their new homes.

One of the areas literary scholars have been diligent in researching and theorizing in the cultural studies of science is the materiality of culture. The materiality of culture has reshaped the way in which people read. George Landow, in his book *Hypertext 2.0: The Convergence of Contemporary Critical Theory and Technology,* points out that at the very moment that deconstruction and poststructuralism are reconfiguring how we think about reading and the text, technologies such as hypertexts are reconfiguring the material dimensions of the book. The hypertext is first and foremost a digitized book that can be printed out but also can be read on the screen. Hypertexts permit readers to take an infinite number of paths to understand the text. For instance, where one begins is an open question, and how one meanders through the book is not dependent on following a linear story guided numerically to the end. Hypertexts have no beginnings or ends. How one understands a text depends on which icons a reader clicks. Each reading of a hypertext is a new reading and a

new book. Hypertexts also change the nature of the relationship between writer and reader. With some hypertexts, the reader can become an author simply by downloading a text, reading it, rewriting certain parts and then uploading it for the original authors and other readers to peruse, thereby activating another chain of events in which the new readers can download, alter, and upload as they please. What kind of story readers can construct from a hypertext is limited only by their imaginations and the sophistication of the technology to permit free reign through the text. With hypertexts, the materiality of reader, author, and text are transformed. The reader and author "morph" into each other, and the text is changed from molecules and atoms on paper to bytes defined by zeros and ones.

Mark Hansen, in his book *Embodying Technesis: Technology beyond Writing*, contends that the shift in the materiality of culture requires a shift to new philosophical and theoretical paradigms. For Hansen, most contemporary theories, whether psychoanalysis, **structuralism**, **deconstruction**, or post-structuralism, privilege the discursive while ignoring what he calls the "robust materiality of technology." Hansen wants to create a philosophical and theoretical perspective that avoids technesis or "the putting-into-discourse" of technology (Hansen, 2000, p. 27). How this robust materiality transforms our thinking and how we relate to the non-discursive dimensions of technology Hansen does not reveal, but it is an issue we have to begin to ponder.

Joseph Tabbi and Michael Wutz view the materiality of culture as an opportunity to explore the ways in which technoscience influences the humanities. They note that "as literature and technology now merge in digital and electronic writing systems, the engineering aesthetics promises to become even more pervasive in the culture" (Tabbi and Wutz, 1997, p. 7). This new engineering aesthetic is the blending of art with technology. It is what R.L. Rutsky calls High Techne. High Techne is best represented in the explosion of animation on the movie screen and the revitalization of comic books. Just as the cultural stud-

---

Structuralism

the belief that underlying all human action from speech to politics are laws that shape the structure of our culture. The role of the intellectual is to uncover these structures.

Deconstruction

a philosophy of reading and thought advocated by Jacques Derrida. In a nutshell, deconstruction is a close reading of texts that opens those texts to other readings and possibilities.

ies of science is breathing new life into literature, technology is revitalizing the arts, creating a new aesthetic that combines the imagination of humans and the mechanical creativity of machines.

A final issue that explains why literary scholars are interested in the materiality of culture and the cultural studies of science is their belief in the human connectedness to material things. As people of books, literary scholars by instinct and training accept the book, no matter what form, as a material thing. The trend, however, in theory and science is to think about the human mind as separate from the body. This book already has discussed this idea in Chapter 1 and in the discussion of the rise of the digital image and Kittler's newest belief that people are entering a posthuman phase in which humans can be "disconnected" from their bodies and the world. Before this shift in his thinking, Kittler demonstrated how individuals were connected to the world in material ways. In his earlier works, Kittler goes back as far as 1800 to demonstrate that with a transformation in technology comes a distinct transformation of the human condition. For example, when the typewriter appeared in the business world, it changed the nature of business administration. Prior to the arrival of the typewriter, most secretaries were men because few women could write. The typewriter changed these conditions as women took advantage of the new technology. As Kittler notes, "women . . . were less oriented toward handwriting and individuality," but through the use of the typewriter "were able to take over this gap in the market by storm, a gap their competitors, mostly male secretaries of the 19th century, overlooked purely out of arrogance" (Kittler, 1997, p. 64). The typewriter became a mechanical means to enter the workforce for women, setting into motion a cultural transformation that eventually would lead to women's right to vote and the right to pursue a career.

The Posthuman Condition

This growing distance between the materiality of culture and scientists' tendencies to ignore the relationships

between human bodies and machines is one of the reasons why more scholars in the cultural studies of science are interested in what is called the posthuman condition. Simply put, the posthuman condition is the merging or morphing of humans with machines or the ability of the organic to extend its life and abilities through the introduction of inorganic materials into their bodies.

Another word often connected to the posthuman condition is **cyborg** or part human, part machine. The number of people who are cyborgs grows every day. Young children on Ritalin or other psychotropic drugs designed to enhance or alter their state of mind are cyborgs. Preschoolers who are immunized before they can enter school are cyborgs. The growing list of young adults who have **cosmetic** and/or **reconstructive** surgery done on their faces, breasts, thighs, calves, or stomachs are cyborgs. Anyone who has received a life-saving transplant, including eyes, is part of the posthuman condition. Anyone who uses Botox injections or who enjoys an enhanced sex life thanks to the drug Viagra is a cyborg. Some scholars suggest that a cyborg is anyone who interacts with others via a computer keyboard. However one defines a cyborg, one should be aware of the serious implications associated with the **posthuman condition**. Chris Gray adroitly summarizes the moral and political implications of some people's choices: "Every year millions of interventions are performed to suck out or insert fat, carve better facial features, modify the immune system, or otherwise 'improve' the natural body. All of these procedures raise important political issues, from the nature of informed consent to the wisdom of using medical resources to improve someone's buttocks while others die for lack of basic care" (Gray, 2001, p. 70).

How did the privileged of the world become posthuman? The history of the posthuman is rooted in Western civilization and the recent developments of computer technology. N. Katherine Hayles and Donna Haraway are two theorists of the posthuman condition.

Hayles believes that the roots of the posthuman condition can be located in early modern thought, especially

Cyborg

something that is part human and part machine and generally, because of this altered condition, healthier and often wealthier than "natural" humans.

Cosmetic Surgery

often refers to unnecessary medical procedures to enhance natural features for vain reasons.

Reconstructive Surgery

refers to the restoration of body features that might have been disfigured at birth or because of an automobile accident or a fire.

in René Descartes' idea that the mind is separate from the body. The origins of the posthuman are also a part of recent technological developments. With the creation of **cybernetics** and **information theory** after World War II, information was privileged over materiality (i.e., the body). Since 1945, many theorists such as Norbert Wiener, Claude Shannon, and Hans Moverec have viewed the body as the original prosthesis. This implies that the body is interchangeable with other bodies and that original parts, whether organs or limbs, can be exchanged for newer and probably better substitutes. Evidence that the body is seen as the original prosthetic can be found in the growth of transplant surgery in the last 20 years and the development of prosthetic limbs that function just like real limbs.

Donna Haraway's "Cyborg Manifesto" is the most famous document describing and charting the rise of the posthuman condition. Originally published in 1985 and reproduced in countless other books, Haraway's essay suggests that the posthuman condition serves as an opportunity to retheorize the political and ascriptive characteristics such as gender, race, and sexual orientation. In "Cyborg Manifesto," Haraway views the rise of the cyborg as the end of essentialism. For instance, if more and more humans are merging with machines to enhance and extend their lives, then what does it mean to be essentially human? In the posthuman world, life is bound to other organisms (e.g., animals) and inorganic materials (e.g., machines). This state of existence is an opportunity for women, especially, to break from the stereotypes that have limited their options. Haraway's cyborg myth is a story in which women are free to enter into careers and relationships that were previously forbidden. However, Haraway is politically savvy enough to note that this new freedom is not a license to continue the modern practice of abusing nature, animals, and machines. Women are not considered superior to men or any other entity of life. The "Cyborg Manifesto" is a call to end the hierarchical ordering of life and the beginning of an era in which all entities are accorded certain rights that ensure their dignity. This includes **neuro-net computers**, artificial life, and artificial intelligence.

Cybernetics

coined by MIT mathematician Norbert Wiener. It literally means "helmsman" and refers to the idea that machines can function just like the human brain as an information-processing device.

Information Theory

refers to the work of Claude Shannon and Warren Weaver. Information theory suggests that meaning is separate from information.

Neuro-net Computers

refers to those computers that function the same way a brain does

Technocultures

Technocultures
computer-mediated relationships between humans. This can include emails, chat lines, or virtual reality simulations.

Immediacy
defined as "a style of visual representation whose goal is to make the viewer forget the presence of the medium" (Bolter and Grusin, 2000, p. 272).

Hypermediacy
a style of visual representation whose goal is to remind the viewer of the medium" (Bolter and Grusin, 2000, p. 272).

Technocultures are computer-mediated interactions between humans who may be next to each other in computer terminals or thousands of miles away in different countries. These interactions can take the form of MUDs (Multi-User Domains), which are usually only text-based, and virtual worlds, which are usually a blend of textual interactions and visual worlds created as the interactions between humans take place. Most visual simulation worlds allow users to create a version of themselves, or avatars, to interact with others in the simulation. These images usually do not look like the real person. The effect of technocultures on society are debated vigorously by scholars.

Jay Bolter and Richard Grusin suggest that technocultures are remediations or reconfigurations of old media forms, especially film. Computer-mediated worlds are guided by two concepts: **immediacy** and **hypermediacy**. Immediacy refers to the belief that the technology we use to create technocultures is most effective when the technology disappears; that is, we do not notice it is there, creating an interactive world for the users. Virtual reality, or VR, is the best contemporary example of immediacy. VR convinces its users through full immersion goggles that what their eyes are experiencing is really in front of them. Sometimes a person playing a virtual reality game may suddenly twirl his or her arms as if about to fall off a cliff. VR users sometimes act in this manner because the vision they experience has them on the edge of a cliff and they really think they are going to fall. This is immediacy at work. Hypermediacy is immediacy's opposite. Hypermediacy is a reminder to technology users that the worlds that people are interacting in are constructed by some technological means. This principle is often used in films or on live television, in which the viewer gets either a shot of a camera filming the movement of an actor or a camera's view of the actor. This is a reminder to viewers that what they are watching is an image and reality constructed by the camera.

Lev Manovich offers another way to understand the effect of technocultures. Technocultures enable users to be "telepresent," which literally means "being present at a distance." Telepresence enables a user to manipulate reality without being physically present. This is what happens every time someone adds to or creates a new avatar for a simulation game or a visual Multi-User Domain. The best image of telepresence is from the movie *Disclosure*, starring Michael Douglas and Demi Moore. Moore plays a high-profile executive in a multinational technology company who claims Douglas has harassed her. In order to show, instead, that Moore has harassed *him* and, moreover, that she is swindling the company, Douglas accesses company files from Thailand from a hotel room in Seattle through a virtual reality system that manages and stores the files on the company online. With the aid of a virtual reality glove and from thousands of miles away, Douglas is able to pull out files, read them, and return them without anyone knowing he viewed them. This is telepresence in action.

Another point to stress in order to understand technocultures is not to assume that computer-generated realities are not real. Pierre Levy suggests that the best comparison to make is between virtualization and actualization. Both concepts represent reality. For Levy, "virtualization is not derealization . . . but a change of identity," or a reality without physical limitations. When people are in a virtual reality system, they are not present in the system, but their interaction with images is projected as a real experience (Levy, 1998, p. 26). Actualization, on the other hand, is "the solution to a problem" (Levy, 1998, p. 25). Actualization is a physical creation. It is this physical dimension that marks virtualization from actualization, but both are real. For example, virtualization is the feeling or belief that one is actually interacting with another person in a Multi-User Domain or on an interactive chat line, while actualization is the actual typing on the keyboard to communicate with other users.

For all the new opportunities that technocultures create, there are also problems associated with these forms of popular culture. David Porter, editor of the book *Internet Culture* suggests that the traditional lore of technocultures

is the belief that they are diverse. Advocates of technocultures argue that users are opened up to many different
experiences and different types of people who think and
act differently from them. Technocultures, the argument
goes, are the ultimate symbol of embracing diversity. Porter
points out, however, that most people who are involved in
technocultures often interact only with those people who
think and act like them. It is true that anyone with the most
unusual interests, such as underwater birthing methods or
homemade space shuttles, can find people on the Internet
with similar interests. Yet people rarely venture beyond
their own interests and interact with those who are different. Porter's point is that technocultures may be the ultimate form of cultural exclusion.

In her book *The War of Desire and Technology at the
Close of the Mechanical Age,* Allucquère (Sandy) Stone
explains the most famous case of Internet abuse. The
urban legend goes that there was a male psychiatrist who
was interested in women's issues. While on the net, he was
able to interact with women, or people who said they were
women, but he would get to a certain point with them,
then they would withdraw. In order to go deeper into their
thoughts, the psychiatrist reintroduced himself as a woman
who was also a psychiatrist who had had an auto accident
that paralyzed her. Women immediately interacted with
the gender-crossing psychiatrist; revealing things that they
never had to her alter, but real, ego. The psychiatrist realized that he had gone too far and started to wonder how
he could get rid of his alternative personality. If he killed
her off, people could be traumatized, and if he told them
who he was, they would feel betrayed. So he decided to
have her come down with a serious illness. People knew
"she" lived in New York, so they began to send flowers to
various New York City hospitals—with no one there to
receive them. Accepting the mess he made, the male psychiatrist finally confessed to his deception. Some women
responded with dismay, others with acceptance, and even
more with the interesting comment, "I should have
known." This special case shows that we often do not know
who we are interacting with in computer-mediated forms

of communication and that essentialist notions of identity are not helpful.

A final example of troubles with technocultures comes from Sherry Turkle. Turkle is a media scholar who is interested in how computer-mediated interactions have changed people's lives. One of the types she discusses in her book, *Life on the Screen,* is a program called Depression 2.0. People with limited resources or with health insurance that will either cover only a few sessions with a psychiatrist or none at all (which is often typical with insurance companies) can seek free advice. Critics argue that a computer cannot make a real diagnosis about whether someone is depressed or not, while advocates argue that health coverage is so expensive and poor in the United States most people are stuck with either getting the advice of a computer program about their state of mind or not getting any help at all.

Science "Wars"

With the development of all these new multidisciplinary fields, the intense interest of literary scholars in science studies, and the rise of technocultures, some scientists have responded with a heightened sense of anxiety. How could someone who is trained in literature or anthropology provide any valuable insight into what scientists do and think? The tension between scholars from the cultural studies of science and practicing scientists exploded on the scene in 1996 when Alan Sokal revealed that his article, "Transgressing the Boundaries: Toward a Transformative Hermeneutics of Quantum Gravity," which he submitted to the cultural studies journal *Social Text,* was a hoax. Immediately, critics of the cultural studies of science interpreted the Sokal hoax as evidence that cultural studies scholars were not capable. Prior to Sokal's fraternity prank, Paul Gross and Norm Levitt came out with their book *Higher Superstition,* claiming that the cultural studies of science represented an attack on reason and scientific knowledge. In 1993, the historian of science Gerald Holton suggested that "anti-science" advocates were a big-

ger threat than "revengeful nationalism, fundamentalism, and ethnic strife" (Holton, 1993, p. 145).

By the end of 1997, the criticisms of the cultural studies of science were mounting and by 1998 were coming from scholars within the field who were nervous that their "serious" work would be dismissed along side of "the weak" work Sokal, Gross, Levitt, and Holton were criticizing. In an article in *A House Built on Sand: Exposing the Postmodernist Myths about Science,* the philosopher of science Philip Kitcher pleaded with his colleagues in the "hard" legitimate sciences not to reject the science studies project because a few "loony ventures styling themselves as contributions to science studies" (Kitcher, 1998, p. 38) are an affront to their scientific sensibilities.

Scholars of the cultural studies of science responded to these criticisms. The editors of the journal *Social Text* suggested that the Sokal hoax does not prove that they do not understand science studies and cannot tell the difference between a legitimate scientific theory and a hoax. Instead, Bruce Robbins suggested that it is a matter of different values. The editors of *Social Text* valued the words of Sokal because they were coming from a practicing scientist, and they trusted that what he was writing about had some basis in reality. One of the goals of the journal *Social Text* is to foster democratic dialogue across numerous constituencies and disciplines in the academic realm. Just as the opinions of graduate students and staff workers are valued in the pages of *Social Text*, so are the voices of scientists, especially those who wish to argue that the debate around scientific theories and funding should be more open to democratic forces.

Other cultural critics of science chimed in as well. Stanley Aronowitz suggested that Sokal and the others were "ill-read and misinformed." There is plenty of evidence to suggest this. For instance, Gross and Levitt dismissed the philosophy of Jacques Derrida because of a statement he made in 1966 at a conference session that was later transcribed concerning the "Einsteinian center," which does not exist. Gerald Holton's comment concerning critics of science being more of a threat than real political strife is widely considered bizarre hyperbole. Roger Hart suggested that the critics of the cultural studies of science were responding with hysterics and rhetorical gimmicks as they were supposedly standing up to defend rational thought and scientific facts. Sharon Traweek, an anthropologist of science, summed up the stakes of these debates when she asked, "Why should there be only one way to think well, only one way to have fun with our minds? Why is mental monogamy required? . . . Does thinking without singularities mean we cannot think carefully about ourselves, other human beings, and our phenomenal world?" (Traweek, 1996, p. 148). This is the heart of the matter. Are there different ways to interpret the truth and understand nature? Are there different ways to think about the effect of science on our understanding of the world that scientists simply refuse to recognize? Why should those who think differently be punished by those who represent one, but not the only, way to think about nature and truth?

Glossary

Cultural Studies of Technoscience is a generic term that includes scholars who are interested in the history, philosophy, sociology, anthropology, and rhetoric of science. Other terms used to describe this interdisciplinary field of study include science studies and science, society, and technology (SST).

Incommensurability is a term Kuhn introduced to suggest that scientific theories represent different cultures, values, beliefs, and laboratory techniques that cannot be compared to each other because of these differences.

Performative and **Instrumental** are terms that refer to the belief that knowledge is not good in and of itself but must enter into an exchange market in which knowledge as information can be exchanged for more valuable goods and services. The rise of the performative university is best highlighted by the growing importance people place on *U.S. News and World Report*'s annual guide to the best universities and colleges. Going to college has become similar to the ranking of college football and basketball teams. The higher the ranking, the belief is, the better the education, and the better the education, the better the job one

will procure in life. The idea of education as a moral endeavor is no longer accepted.

Structuralism is the belief that underlying all human action from speech to politics are laws that shape the structure of our culture. The role of the intellectual is to uncover these structures.

Deconstruction is a philosophy of reading and thought advocated by Jacques Derrida. In a nutshell, deconstruction is a close reading of texts that opens those texts to other readings and possibilities.

Cyborg is part human, part machine and, because of this altered condition, generally healthier and often wealthier than "natural" humans.

Cosmetic Surgery often refers to unnecessary medical procedures done to enhance natural features for vanity.

Reconstructive Surgery refers to the restoration of body features that might have been disfigured at birth or because of an automobile accident or fire.

Cybernetics was coined by the MIT mathematician Norbert Wiener. It literally means "helmsman" and refers to the idea that machines can function just like the human brain as an information processing device.

Information Theory refers to the work of Claude Shannon and Warren Weaver. Information theory suggests that meaning is separate from information.

Neuro-net Computers refers to those computers that function the same way a brain does

Technocultures are computer-mediated relationships between humans. This can include emails, chat lines, and virtual reality simulations.

Immediacy is defined as "a style of visual represenation whose goal is to make the viewer forget the presence of the medium" (Bolter and Grusin, 2000, p. 272).

Hypermediacy is "a style of visual representation whose goal is to remind the viewer of the medium" (Bolter and Grusin, 2000, p. 272).

Cultural Studies of/in Education

This final chapter will cover the cultural studies of education. This scholarship is not a long tradition (25 years), but it is important to look at some of the early pathfinding work that has emerged. After a discussion of the "trailblazers," this chapter will break down the cultural studies of education into fields of interest that cover such topics as childhood studies, critical media literacy, critical pedagogy, and cultural curriculum studies.

Early Works in the Cultural Studies of Education

In an interview he conducted with Lawrence Grossberg, Handel Wright framed his interactions with the acknowledgment that "education has not featured particularly prominently in the international cultural studies discourse, especially in North America. On the other hand, until quite recently education in North America had not exactly embraced cultural studies either" (Wright, 2000, p. 1). Wright's comments were appropriate and accurate observations, especially within the context of interviewing

Grossberg, one of the few scholars, along with Angela Mcrobbie and Paul Willis, to address pedagogical issues. Wright is also correct to point out the disinterest in popular culture among most educators. To date, major educational journals such as *American Educational Research Journal* (AERJ) and *Teacher's College Record* have simply ignored popular culture and its effect on schooling, while other journals such as *Harvard Educational Review* are just beginning to discover popular culture. With the exception of Valerie Walkerdine, there are few educational psychologists interested in popular culture, no one in educational leadership writing about popular culture, and absolutely little interest in the field of educational statistics. These are the major fields in education. Most scholars interested in the cultural studies of education are marginalized or they conduct their research under the umbrella of another field, such as foundations of education or literacy. This is not an uncommon phenomenon. Cultural studies in other fields, such as literature, is often conducted by scholars who already have established their names in their respective fields, such as Andrew Ross in poetry, Cary Nelson in academic work and literature, and Bruce Robbins in comparative literature.

It should not be much of surprise that major journals within the field of education have only entered into the discourses of cultural studies at this junction because the history of ideas suggests that radical changes in thinking and academic work rarely, if ever, comes from established fields of knowledge or elite universities. For instance, computer science as a field of study did not emerge as a legitimate discipline in elite universities such as Harvard or Yale but rather in places such as the University of Washington. Once a field is established, then well-endowed universities create their departments by raiding the those that took the risks.

If cultural studies is a relatively new discourse in education, it is strengthened by its investments in multiple theoretical traditions. In the same interview with Wright, Grossberg noted that one of the hallmarks of cultural studies is that "people make different levels of investment in different theoretical positions: they read differentially" (Wright, 2000, p. 7). To some, this differential reading of theory and culture may seem to be a statement of disarray and chaos, but in reality it represents a nascent state of intellectual growth in which educational scholars are probing to find out which cultural studies traditions are most fruitful. Given time, the traditions of cultural studies will be as strong in education as they are in literature, communications, and the sciences.

When discussing the importance of cultural studies in education, one needs to begin with the work of Paul Willis. Willis in 1977 published an ethnographic study of working-class males in England. He was interested in how working-class males formulate their own cultures and resist the dominant culture. Willis concluded that the working-class males rightly interpreted the schooling process as one of the major institutions that the ruling class used to **reproduce** the status quo. He noted that in an ironic twist the males were astute enough to realize that the primary function of schools was to prepare them for work and to accept the class system that favored the wealthy and ruling classes. However, these young "lads" did not realize that their **resistance** to education cemented their position as workers and prevented them from challenging or entering into the ruling classes. This is exactly what the ruling classes wanted. The ruling classes wanted to make sure, Willis noted, that "the same standards, ideologies, and aspirations [were] not really passed on to all." If schools followed their equalitarian ethos, it would prove "catastrophic for social reproduction in general" (Willis, 1977, p. 177).

Another study that established the roots of cultural studies in education, but which is usually ignored, is the work edited by Leslie Roman and Linda Christian-Smith *Becoming Feminine: The Politics of Popular Culture*. They addressed two major themes in this study: 1) how popular culture shapes the identities of young women and 2) how the academic discourse and theorizing of popular culture is a male discourse. Roman and Christian-Smith's work offers an alternative to a male-dominated discourse that

Reproduce or Reproduction refers to the idea that societies, democratic or not, use institutions such as schools, universities, churches, and popular entertainment to reaffirm the values, tastes, and beliefs of those in power.

Resistance the idea that in order to challenge dominant cultures, disenfranchised groups create their own cultures. This has taken the form of working-class cultures, youth cultures, and fan cultures.

treats "popular cultural forms and their gender ideologies as *constructs* subject to undoing or deconstruction" (Roman and Christian-Smith, 1988, p. 21). From this undoing, they wished to offer their own interpretations and readings of popular culture in a manner that would not subordinate the identities of women to males and the voices of academic researchers.

Yet another scholar who was an early explorer of cultural studies and education is Henry Giroux. Unlike Willis, Roman, and Christian-Smith, Giroux does not come from an anthropological tradition. Instead, he has combined the Frankfurt tradition (corporate influences on popular entertainment), the work of Paulo Freire (education as a democratic endeavor), and traditional cultural criticism (textual analysis). Giroux is known for his ability to combine a stinging criticism of the corporate influence on popular culture tastes while offering a distinct alternative to corporate popular culture that fosters the development of democratic ideals in schools and popular culture. With this combination of critique and hope, Giroux has been able to provide insightful commentaries on topics ranging from the effect of Disney on childhood to beauty pageants and how films and television shape how young people think about and act within society. Giroux's approach has its drawbacks, however. Rarely does one read in Giroux's work the voices of the young people he theorizes. As with the Frankfurt School, Giroux's primary focus on the effect of the "culture industry" in the creation of popular culture constructs young people as objects who cannot react or interact but can only be manipulated by popular culture. In spite of this limitation, Giroux has made a career in trying to construct a public space in which "education is affirmed as a political process that encourages people to identify themselves as more than consuming subjects and democracy as more than a spectacle of market culture" (Giroux, 2000, p. 105).

Childhood Studies and Consuming Children

Childhood studies is one of the most fascinating contributions educational scholars have made to cultural studies. Childhood studies is markedly different from traditional approaches to adolescents in numerous ways. Scholars in this field reject most of what developmental psychologists say about children, especially the linear and modernist notion that children grow in progressive stages. The most important effect that childhood studies has had on the study of adolescents is the primary focus on the myriad ways corporations now shape the identities and affective tastes of young people. From Beanie Babies to Disney to McDonalds to foster care as a profit-making business, childhood studies scholars have demonstrated how a corporate ethos has shaped and infected the thinking of young people.

Like most fields of study, it is difficult to pinpoint when scholars began to study the intersection between childhood and popular culture. Even so, two of the major contributions among many are Shirley Steinberg and Joe Kincheloe's work *Kinderculture: The Corporate Construction of Childhood* and Gaile Cannella and Joe Kincheloe's book *Kidworld: Childhood Studies, Global Perspective, and Education*. Steinberg and Kincheloe suggest that one of the purposes of childhood studies is to understand what it means to grow up in a postmodern, hypermediated, unrelenting corporatized world. They conclude that the corporatizing of childhood undermines almost everything parents value. "Contemporary children's access to commercial kinderculture and popular culture," Steinberg and Kincheloe suggest, "not only motivates them to become hedonistic consumers but also undermines the innocence, the protected status from the tribulations of adult existence" parents have tried to foster (Steinberg and Kincheloe, 1997, p. 16). This impact is decisive and devastating. Parents no longer raise their children alone. McDonald's play places, Nintendo playstations, surrogate nannies (television and movies) complete with entertaining advertisements, and fashionable icons in music and dress educate today's children. The great thing for corporations is they can fill children with any kind of images and ideas with little or no responsibility. One's the realities and impacts of consumer

values and ethics. This responsibility to explain the seductive power of corporate culture, ironically, is about the only thing parents are expected to do. It is the parents' job to explain to the young person that, after spending hours hearing they can have everything, they actually cannot have everything. This reality is a modern tale of Dickens' *The Christmas Carol* in which corporations are Santa Claus (although this one is less altruistic and demands to be paid) and the parents are Scrooges.

Scholars within the field of childhood studies have begun to not only critique the amoral and nihilistic tendencies of corporate culture. They offer an alternative that does not strive to return to a **nostalgic** era when parents were in complete control of their children's development. Childhood scholars offer proactive approaches for teachers, parents, and young people to counteract the influences of a corporatized world. Gaile Cannella suggests that educational scholars should begin to give young people voices in the research we conduct and the policies we advocate. This approach will open the door to the analysis of "contemporary issues and actual material conditions that have been imposed on those who are younger and tied to concepts of 'child'" (Cannella and Kincheloe, 2002, p. 10). Once young people are invited into a dialogue about education and the material conditions of their lives, one hopes, they will begin to openly critique what corporations have irresponsibly been feeding them as desirable and unlimited. Young people will not necessarily reject corporate culture, but they will perhaps begin to hold corporations responsible for the worlds they try to create and the marks they leave on the young.

Without a doubt the most influential ethos that corporations have instilled in the minds of young people and adults is the will to consume. Corporations in most Western societies have constructed a discourse that suggests to everyone within listening distance of a television, CD player, movie theater, or radio that one's identity is shaped by consumption and anyone who cannot consume at an acceptable rate is not a worthy member of modern society. When it comes to constructing a consumption

Nostalgic

refers to a person who believes a previous time was more pristine and idyllic than the current era. The word "nostalgia" literally means "a yearning for a time that never existed."

ethic, corporations have been unrelenting and immoral. Corporations have taken an interest in advertising in schools and developing curricula in schools in order to construct future loyal customers. Research suggests that the tastes of individuals can be shaped and developed as early as two years old and further research suggests that if corporations are successful at an early age they can develop a brand loyalty that usually lasts a lifetime. In this sense, schools have not become sites of educating future citizens of democracies, but rather they have become sites of educating future workers who live to consume. To many this may not sound like a grave threat to the development of young people, and to many young people it may not sound like a bad purpose for schools. However, the impact the consumption ethos has on the future of democratic governments and the intellectual development of individuals is serious.

One the most important studies on the impact of consumption and young people is Jane Kenway and Elizabeth Bullen's work *Consuming Children: Education-Entertainment-Advertising*. They chart the ways in which young people have been recast as untapped markets and the curricula of the schools are seen as the first public relations opportunity to affect the way young people think about a corporation. As a result, Burger King, Taco Bell, and Pizza Hut have made major inroads in offering their "food" in cafeterias, Coke and Pepsi have struck deals to offer their products in vending machines, and Exxon has created an environmental curriculum to counteract its tarnished image after the *Valdez* oil spill off the coast of Alaska. Cash-strapped schools, of course, are not innocent victims in this tale of corporate raiding of young people's minds. Each time a corporation "donates" athletic gear or curriculum material, the school benefits either with a direct cash influx or with the reduced burden of spending taxpayer money to purchase new sports uniforms or textbooks. However, the students often pay a high price. They are commodified as school property that can be sold to corporations in exchange for cash.

Kenway and Bullen, however, are clear that the impact

of this invasion into schools has numerous consequences. Advertising that is now common in most public schools stunts the critical abilities of young people, especially in those schools that do not offer a media literacy program where corporate actions can be studied. In their study, Kenway and Bullen concur with Brian Young when he concludes that "advertising is a particular form of discourse where only the best side of a case is put forward so that the virtues of the topic are presented, to the relative neglect of the vices" (Kenway and Bullen, 2001, p. 30). Moreover, corporate culture reinvents young people into "the consuming child of the West" that purposively ignores the "highly exploitative sweatshop production of young children" in other nations (Kenway and Bullen, 2001, p. 37).

Kenway and Bullen offer plenty of advice as to what schools and young people can do to counteract corporate culture and consuming children. Young people can follow some of their peers who have not accepted the notion of the passive consumer and taken the images and ideas of corporations to reconfigure and redefine them to reclaim the public space of schools and enter into a dialogue over the detrimental effects of child labor and mindless consumption. Kenway and Bullen suggest that young people become a "cyberflâneur . . . who transgresses the spatial, physical, and temporal boundary of the corporate world through technology" (Kenway and Bullen, 2001, p. 178). This cyberinteraction permits young people the opportunity to interact with other young people who might see the world of consumption differently and together they may begin to change their attitudes about corporate culture and take back their schools in order to transform them into sites of critical dialogue and intellectual growth.

Yet another voice against the corporatization of schools is Peter McLaren. McLaren views consumerism as a form of predatory culture. Predatory culture "is the great deceiver" filled with "eroticized victims and decaffeinated revolutionaries." Predatory culture marks an implosion of our existence in which the "social, the cultural, and the human has been subsumed within capital" (McLaren, 1995, p. 2). To counteract the seductiveness of predatory

Critical Pedagogy
an alternative approach to learning that centers the curriculum around the experiences and history of students and teachers.

culture, McLaren seeks to create a **critical pedagogy** that permits students to become actors in history rather than passive conduits of makeshift, revisionist history that covers up the scandalized version constructed in the corporate and entertainment worlds. Students have to assert themselves into history in order to construct their own identities since there are numerous others who wish to define their existence as future workers and consumers.

Critical Media Literacy

One of the major contributions educational scholars have made to cultural studies is a call for the creation of a media literacy program in schools. As mentioned in Chapter 1, to understand popular culture one has to understand how images shape our reality. Scholars who advocate a critical media literacy take this contention one step further. Critical media literacy recognizes that images do not represent reality but shape and define reality. The impact of popular culture images is more profound than the written word and more influential in shaping what people accept as truth. For example, Oliver Stone in his film *JFK* presented a theory that Lee Harvey Oswald could not have been the lone assassin of Kennedy. Stone was able to construct an effective interpretation of the JFK assassination by placing his own film frames into original frames of the assassination. Viewers, especially those who were not born in 1963, came away with the impression that they actually saw more than one gunman.

Critical media literacy scholars suggest that schools should either offer classes that specifically address the many ways in which images influence and construct reality or schools should integrate media literacy into their current curricula. Whichever approach schools choose, critical media literacy requires schools to do two things. First, school curricula should offer students the opportunity to critique multimedia sources so they can see how images construct reality and understand how they can critique images. Second, schools should offer media sources as a supplement to written documents. For instance, if students are going to read about the Holocaust they should

also see *Schindler's List* or *The Pianist*, or if they are going to read Shakespeare they should also view the current screen versions of Shakespeare's *Romeo and Juliet*, *Hamlet*, or *A Midsummer Night's Dream*. Students, however, should do more than just watch and conclude that the movie was better than the text. Students should also learn how each medium is different and how each medium presents reality. A film should not be dismissed because it is different from the novel but students should learn how the medium of film requires that a novel be presented differently.

Scholars have debated the difference between popular culture media (i.e., films and television) and traditional media favored in schools (i.e., the textbook). Robert Rosenstone is the leading scholar in this field. He suggests that because the medium of film is inherently different from the written word, films cannot tell a story in the same way a book does. Focusing primarily on historically based films, Rosenstone reminds his readers that no matter what the medium is, the words we read or the images we see are not the past but representations of the past, and these representations make the past something that comes alive only through the words on a page or images on a screen. The main point Rosenstone makes about these two media is that, whereas a book has an unlimited number of pages to tell a story, films are generally limited to between 90 and 200 minutes. Given this disadvantage in telling the stories of the past, filmmakers have to use certain techniques to overcome their temporal limitations. The main concept that filmmakers use is **condensation**. Condensation takes numerous historical characters and condenses them into one character, or takes numerous events and creates one event to explain them. This saves time in having to introduce and develop numerous characters or represent numerous events in a short time frame. Condensation changes the way the past is represented, but it does not imply that films are less accurate than books in representing history.

Brian Goldfarb also sees a difference between the written word and images. Goldfarb suggests that we need

Condensation
a "highly selected and condensed sample of what could be included" in a historical film (Rosenstone, 1995, p. 144).

Visual Pedagogy
an active approach to understanding how visual images shape our reality and how we can be active in this construction of reality, especially as it applies to our race, gender, and sexual orientation.

to create a **visual pedagogy**. A visual pedagogy recognizes that we live in a visual world in which images bombard our minds every day. Goldfarb's main contribution to the discussion is his advocacy for students as media creators. All schools, he believes, should acquire media equipment so students can go out and learn how to produce films and videos. When students produce films and videos, they interact with images and begin an engagement process that raises "questions of agency, authority, and knowledge production" (Goldfarb, 2002, p. 13).

Other scholars recognize the potential of images to educate. In the book *Popular Culture and Critical Pedagogy*, edited by Toby Daspit and the author of this book, John Weaver, one of the main points is that many forms of popular culture are stellar examples of critical pedagogy at work. The editors demonstrate how students and teachers take such popular culture icons as *The Simpsons, Roseanne,* and hip-hop music to create a critical understanding of what people are experiencing in the world. For instance, critical theorists argue that schools should become places where students question the world and act as agents in the world in order to change it. The editors contend that many popular culture forms do just that. *The Simpsons* presents a view of schooling that is bleak but that also shows how schools can be sites for learning. The literary critic Houston Baker also makes similar claims when he suggests that Shakespeare was the first rapper. Baker chronicles how he took his idea to a working-class school in England. The headmaster of the school apologized to him before he met the students who, according to the headmaster, would be disengaged and disinterested in what he had to say. However, the students were enthralled with Baker's ideas that Shakespeare could rap. One student even asked to return to Philadelphia with him so he could learn more about the connections between rap and Shakespeare.

Cultural Curriculum Studies

William Reynolds who coined the term "cultural curriculum studies." It recognizes that if we are interested in

Curriculum Theory
a branch of curriculum fostered by William Pinar, Madeleine Grumet, Dwayne Hubner, and James MacDonald that stresses the need to abandon the Tylerian design approach to curriculum development.

Hermeneutics
literally means "to interpret." In curriculum theory hermeneutics is a way to interpret the possible meanings of educational discourses.

the ideas, identities, and learning habits of young people, we cannot avoid the effect of popular culture. For Reynolds, **curriculum theory** and cultural studies both approach knowledge in a multidisciplinary way and both are interested in the impact of popular culture on our lives. Yet the conversation between the two groups has only begun. One of the reasons the conversation between cultural studies and curriculum theory has only begun is that, like most other fields within education, popular culture was ignored until the 1980s.

William Reynolds' work is an important place to start when discussing the meaning of cultural curriculum studies. Originally interested in **hermeneutics** in curriculum theory, Reynolds began a shift in his thinking in the early 1990s concerning the importance of popular culture in curriculum issues. Like most educational scholars, film is the predominant mode of interest in Reynold's work. Reynolds is interested in how films project images of schools as sites for control, surveillance, and reproduction. These issues manifest themselves in many ways in films and often construct the meaning of the schooling process. For instance, in most films, the schooling process is depicted in private schools as tightly controlled by traditionalists who know what it takes to get their students into the Ivy League schools or, in the case of the film *Mona Lisa Smile*, married to Ivy League students. The students and teachers in these films (e.g., *Dead Poets Society, School Ties,* and *The Emperor's Club*) are constructed as repressed figures suffering from the strict traditions of elite schools, but their talents emerge in the end as they ready themselves to change the world. Public schools are depicted differently. Most public schools in films (e.g., *Lean On Me, Teachers,* and *The Faculty*) are constructed as urban or even suburban jungles where students are ready to pounce on law-biding but unsuspecting adults. If students are not pathologized in these films, they are usually depicted as rays of hope that eventually are tragically trampled by the "unruly" factions within the public schools.

There are other scholars who have shaped the discourse around cultural curriculum studies, including

Susan Edgerton and Peter Appelbaum. In her study *Translating the Curriculum: Multiculturalism into Cultural Studies*, Edgerton demonstrates how cultural studies informs how we can rethink school curricula. She demonstrates that cultural studies is a way to tie the experiences of students with the experiences of schooling: certainly not an easy task. Yet Edgerton writes of ways in which her students have been able to make connections with course content that they never experienced in other classes. Her students left her class educationally resuscitated while eager to take part in changing society when it came to such varied issues as race and incarceration, history and ignored social groups, and the use of textbooks as opposed to more reliable and detailed documents in teaching young people.

Peter Appelbaum's work is based on this premise: How can we incorporate the ideas of our students into our curriculum plans? Appelbaum demonstrates through popular culture that it is easy to do this. For instance, in his work Appelbaum asked elementary school students how teachers could use the story lines of Saturday morning cartoons in their curricula. Appelbaum then took these ideas to the teachers. Some of the teachers incorporated the ideas into their weekly plans, but for the most part the teachers were uncertain what to do with them. Appelbaum reported that the main reason teachers were uncertain is that they wanted Appelbaum to tell them how to think about their students' ideas. These teachers believed, Appelbaum noted, that ideas should come from professors, teachers should implement them, and students should learn the material. Within this approach, popular culture will rarely ever be incorporated into the curriculum because it does not symbolize legitimate knowledge. Yet in his work on mathematics and science education, Appelbaum has shown how popular culture is ripe with material that can demonstrate mathematical and scientific ideas at work.

When discussing cultural curriculum studies, the work of Noel Gough is essential. In his work *Laboratories in Fiction*, it is Gough's contention that if teachers want to teach science well they should abandon textbooks, which

is not an uncommon practice, and use popular culture sources such as comic books, science fiction, and music. Gough demonstrates that comic books do a better job of relating the latest scientific ideas to students than textbooks. Most science textbooks in high schools, and even in universities, stop at 1900 and Max Planck's discoveries with quantum physics. While Newtonian principles of science still apply to many areas of physics, ignoring the last 100 years of science erases the importance of quantum physics, chaos, and complexity theories as well as biotechnology issues. Comic books, on the other hand, present students with an understanding of contemporary theories.

Another argument Gough makes is that science fiction is a great source for science teachers. This is a similar argument made in the book *Science Fiction Curriculum, Cyborg Teachers, and Youth Cultures*, edited by Karen Anijar, Toby Daspit, and the author of this book, John Weaver. The editors contend that science fiction is an important way to teach science and to broach many other important issues in schools. For instance, the work of Octavia Butler is an important source to discuss gender and sexual orientation issues in literature class. In her fiction, Butler discusses environmental issues in which humans are often forced to flee their decimated planet, move to other solar systems, and, in order to survive, intermingle with different intergalactic species. This is Butler's way of discussing same-sex marriages and interracial relationships. Yet another example is the work of H.G. Wells to discuss such issues as Einstein's general and special theory of relativity, the fourth dimension of space, and the issue of time travel.

There is a price, of course, for advocating such approaches to teaching and learning. The science fiction critic Marleen Barr embodies this risk. In her book *Lost in Space: Probing Feminist Science Fiction and Beyond* describes how writing about science fiction as an academic career can be risky for tenure and promotion. She notes that "the danger of unknowingly obeying patriarchal traffic signals [i.e., males telling female academics what is a legitimate topic to write about or teach] . . . was more onerous to me than the risk of being denied tenure for choosing the 'wrong' field of study" (Barr, 1993, p. 4). Barr was denied tenure. As her case depicts, the price of teaching and thinking differently can be high, but, as Appelbaum, Edgerton, and Gough demonstrate, it can also be the most rewarding experience for teachers and students alike. Science fiction reminds us what curriculum theory can be and what schooling should be.

One final person to mention in cultural curriculum studies is Greg Dimitriadis. Dimitriadis' work is different from most curriculum theory scholars. While he was a doctoral student, Dimitriadis conducted a four-year study of African American youth in a small Midwest urban setting. Among other issues, he was interested in how youth appropriated popular culture texts to make meaning and sense of a world that seemed to be openly hostile to them. Dimitriadis's work represents an anthropological approach to cultural studies that connects with Paul Willis' work in the field. One of the most interesting dimensions of Dimitriadis' work is how he shows that young people read popular culture. The youth that he interacted with were very much interested in hip-hop. Hip-hop helped them understand their identities not only as African Ameican youth but, for some of them, as Southern transplants to the Midwest region. Southern rap spoke to and often for them as they were trying to understand why capitalist America showed little interest in their plights as young people growing up in the United States. Another dimension that hip-hop provided in the lives of these young people was lively debate. Dimitriadis demonstrates how these young people were interested in the issue of whether Tupac Shakur was really dead or not. Tupac is this generation's Elvis: a person who represented their dreams, hopes, and fears, and since his alleged demise he has risen to an iconic status. Dimitriadis's work has filled in an important gap in the work of curriculum theorists, and through his ethnographical work has offered numerous suggestions for policymakers and those interested in working with young people in urban areas.

The Future of Cultural Studies in Education

If educational fields of knowledge are to remain relevant, more scholars will have to begin to account for the effect of poplar culture on the learning experiences of students and teachers. This means educational psychologists, statisticians, administrators, and curriculum scholars will have to recognize the importance of popular culture in their research. They will also have to move beyond superficial issues such as how many scenes of violence the average child views on television. Popular culture is much more sophisticated in its ability to teach young people and adults what and how to think. Rarely, if ever, does television or any form of popular culture cause violence. It can fuel the creative faculties of a disturbed young person, but focusing on what influences the imagination does not address what triggers a person to act violently. A healthy approach to popular culture and education would develop a pedagogy that utilizes the power of popular culture in order to enhance democracy. Popular culture serves as a forum to raise issues that are of concern for young people, and schools should permit these issues to be developed within the confines of daily school activities. The cultural studies of education can play a vital role in creating new approaches to learning that invite young people and their cultures into the dialogue about what knowledge matters most. Such an approach to learning need not be done at the expense of eliminating traditional subjects but rather popular culture can be incorporated into the current curricula core subjects. This primer has tried to show how cultural studies and popular culture address such issues as science education, history, literature, and art. Moreover, this book has tried to show that in order to understand the importance of popular culture in our lives, we should understand how images affect our thinking, and how media technically work to re-present and construct reality.

Glossary

Reproduce or **Reproduction** refers to the idea that societies, democratic or not, use institutions such as schools, univer-

sities, churches, and popular entertainment to reaffirm the values, tastes, and beliefs of those in power.

Resistance is the idea that in order to challenge dominant cultures, disenfranchised groups create their own cultures. This has taken the form of working-class cultures, youth cultures, and fan cultures.

Nostalgic refers to a person who believes a previous time period was more pristine and idyllic than the current era. The word "nostalgia" literally means a yearning for a time that never existed.

Critical Pedagogy is an alternative approach to learning that centers the curriculum around the experiences and history of the students and teachers. Critical pedagogy also encourages students and teachers to take an active role in the creation of political and social movements and policy-making.

Condensation is a "highly selected and condensed sample of what could be included" in a historical film. (Rosenstone, 1995, p. 144).

Visual Pedagogy is an active approach to understanding how visual images shape our reality and how we can be active in this construction of reality, especially as it applies to our race, gender, and sexual orientation.

Curriculum Theory is a branch of curriculum fostered by William Pinar, Madeleine Grumet, Dwayne Hubner, and James MacDonald that stresses the need to abandon the Tylerian design approach to curriculum development while favoring more sociological, psychological, philosophical, and historical dimensions of curriculum and its effect on teachers and students.

Hermeneutics literally means to interpret. In curriculum theory, hermeneutics is a way to interpret the possible meanings of educational discourses.

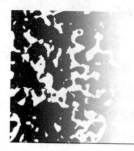

Suggested Readings

This is the most important chapter of the primer. This primer should serve not as a textbook but an introduction whereby students of education might continue their reading. If this book is read like a textbook, then the author will have failed in the book's primary goal—to encourage further and deeper reading in the field of cultural studies. Like many scholars, this author believes that textbooks have "dumbed down" and numbed the intellectual process. Like Douglas Aoki, this author believes that textbooks aim to communicate "knowledge but doing so in a standard and universal way: to replicate itself in the mind of its every reader" (*Journal of Curriculum Theory*, 2002, 18:1, pp. 21–39). Textbooks have become substitutes for reading primary sources. The intention in this chapter is to provide readers with as many primary sources as possible so the intellectual journey can be as fruitful and challenging as possible without settling for the poor substitute called textbooks.

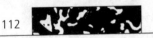

Further Readings for Chapter 1

On the history of popular culture and the invention of the concept of Culture, Plato's *Republic*, edited by Alan Bloom (1968, Basic Books), is essential reading in order to understand where contemporary criticisms of popular culture developed. If one wants to develop an understanding of the idea of culture and the liberal-arts education in the Western world, it is important to read Kant's *The Conflict of the Faculties* (Mary Gregor, translator, 1978, University of Nebraska Press), Matthew Arnold's classic study *Culture and Anarchy* (Samuel Lipman, editor, 1994, Yale University Press), F.R. Leavis' *The Critic as Anti-Philosopher* (1982, Elephant Paperbacks), Leo Strauss' essays on liberalism found in *Liberalism: Ancient and Modern* (1968, University of Chicago Press), and Alan Bloom's contemporary rant *The Closing of the American Mind* (1988, Simon & Schuster). Helpful critiques of Kant's *The Conflict of the Faculties* can be found in Peggy Kamuf's *The Division of Literature or the University in Deconstruction* (1997, University of Chicago Press) and *Logomachia: The Conflict of the Faculties* (Richard Rant, editor, 1992, University of Nebraska Press). Alan Bloom's work has created a cottage industry of replies to his allegations about the contemporary university. Of note is Lawrence Levine's thoughtful response, fittingly entitled *The Opening of the American Mind* (1996, Beacon Press). The most insightful commentary on Arnold's idea is Richard Miller's work *As if Learning Matters: Reforming Higher Education* (1998, Cornell University Press).

The most important scholar in understanding the meaning of images is W.J.T. Mitchell. In order to get the most comprehensive history of images, one should read Mitchell's *Iconology: Image, Text, Ideology* (1986, University of Chicago Press) and the sequel, *Picture Theory* (1994, University of Chicago Press). For anyone interested in the intellectual history of images in the Western world, Mitchell provides numerous connections and references to the two most important figures in the field: Erwin Panofsky and Ernst Gombrich. Another indispensable text for understanding the history of images is J. Hillis Miller's work

Illustration (1992, Harvard University Press). The classic text regarding the film image is Jacques Aumont's *The Image* (1997, British Film Institute Publishing) and the edited work translated by Richard Neupert, *Aesthetics of Film: Jacques Aumont, Alain Bergala, Michel Marie, and Marc Vernet* (1992, University of Texas at Austin Press).

The literature on the digital image is abundant and intriguing. For anyone interested in the technological and aesthetic meaning of the digital image, as well as other new media, Lev Manovich's book *The Language of New Media* (2001, MIT Press) is essential. Mark Hansen's work is also important in understanding the philosophical meanings of the digital image. His first book, *Embodying Technesis: Technology beyond Writing* (2000, University of Michigan Press), offers a detailed history of Western intellectual thinking on technology. One should also read his recent articles on the topic of the digital image: "The Affective Topology of New Media Art" (*Spectator* 21:1, 2001, pp. 40–70) and "Cinema beyond Cybernetics or How to Frame the Digital Image" (*Configurations* 10, 2003, pp. 51–90). Friedrich Kittler is an important historian and philosopher of media as well. His best-known works include *Discourse Networks, 1800/1900* (1990, Stanford University Press), *Gramaphone, Film, Typewriter* (Geoffrey Winthrop-Young and Michael Wutz, translators, 1999, Stanford University Press), and *Literature Media, Information Systems* (John Johnston, translators, 1997, G+B Arts Publishers). Anyone interested in his unconventional views of the posthuman and digital image should read his article "Computer Graphics: A Semi-Technical Introduction" (*Grey Room* 2, 2001, pp. 30–45).

For a general understanding of the effect of digital images on popular culture and society, readers should see Pierre Levy's *Becoming Virtual: Reality in the Digital Age* (Robort Bononno, translators, 1998, Plenum Trade Publishers), and R.L. Rutsky's splendid and insightful *High Techne: Art and Technology from the Machine Aesthetic to the Posthuman* (1999, University of Minnesota Press). For an understanding of digital images and photography, William J. Mitchell's *The Reconfigured Eye: Visual*

Truth in the Post-Photographic Era (1992, MIT Press) is the best starting point. Andrew Darley, in *Visual Digital Culture: Surface Play and Spectacle in the New Media Genres* (2000, Routledge), offers a look into the many ways digital technology is influencing films, music videos, and computer games. Read Catherine Waldby's *The Visible Human Project* (2000, Routledge) to understand the many ways in which digital images are influencing medicine and science.

Further Readings for Chapter 2

On defining cultural studies, see J. Hillis Miller's book *Illustration* (1992, Harvard University Press). To understand the different nationalistic approaches to cultural studies, see the collection edited by David Morley and Kevin Robins entitled *British Cultural Studies* (2001, Oxford University Press); the reader edited by Houston Baker Jr., Manthia Diawara, and Ruth Lindeborg, *Black British Cultural Studies: A Reader* (1996, University of Chicago Press); the collection edited by Scott Denham, Irene Kacandes, and Jonathan Petropoulos entitled *A User's Guide to German Cultural Studies* (1997, University of Michigan Press); the reader edited by John Frow and Meaghan Morris, *Australian Cultural Studies: A Reader* (1993, University of Illinois Press); Graeme Turner's *Nation, Culture, Text: Australian Cultural and Media Studies* (1993, Routledge); the collection edited by Sian Reynolds and William Kidd *Contemporary French Cultural Studies* (2000, Edward Arnold Publishers); and for the United States Alan Trachtenberg's series *Cultural Studies in the United States* (University of North Carolina Press).

The literature on the Frankfurt School is impressive. For those interested in the intellectual history of the Frankfurt School, Martin Jay's work, *The Dialectical Imagination: A History of the Frankfurt School and the Institute of Social Research, 1923–1950* (1974, University of California Press, with a 1998 edition as well) is still the quintessential source. Jay is also the author of an intellectual biography of Theodore Adorno, aptly titled *Adorno* (1984, Harvard University Press). Adorno and Max Horkheimer's "Culture Industry" article can be found in *The Dialectic of Enlightenment* (originally published in English in 1972 and reissued in 1998 by Continuum Publishing Company).

Walter Benjamin's "Art in the Age of Mechanical Reproduction" can be found in a collection of his essays titled *Illuminations* (1969, Schocken Press, pp. 217–251). To understand Benjamin and the significance of his work, Miriam Bratu Hansen's work is essential. Her articles "Benjamin and Cinema: Not a One-Way Street" (*Critical Inquiry* 25:2, pp. 306–343) and "Of Mice and Ducks: Benjamin and Adorno on Disney" (*South Atlantic Quarterly* 92:1, pp. 27–61). In the *Critical Inquiry* issue, one can also find careful and illuminating works on Benjamin from Geoffrey Hartman ("Benjamin in Hope," pp. 344–352) and Shoshana Felman ("Benjamin's Silence," pp. 201–234). There are also helpful essays on Benjamin in Gary Smith's edited work, *On Walter Benjamin: Critical Essays and Recollections* (1991, MIT Press).

For those interested in the traditions of cultural criticism in the United States, there is no better place to begin than with Gilbert Seldes' works. *The Seven Lively Arts* (originally published in 1924 and reissued in 1957, A.S. Barnes and Company) is the first major attempt in the United States to critically defend popular culture. Seldes also published a collection of his essays later in his career that includes television, entitled *The Public Arts* (1956, Simon and Schuster). In these essays, Seldes offers early insights into the development of television and his role as program director for CBS. Michael Kammen has written a wonderful biography on Seldes, *The Lively Arts: Gilbert Seldes and the Transformation of Cultural Criticism in the United States* (1996, Oxford University Press). Besides Seldes, Parker Tyler was an early popular culture critic. His work focuses on movies from a psychoanalytical approach. *The Hollywood Hallucination* (1944, Simon and Schuster) and *Magic and Myth of the Movies* (1947, Henry Holt and

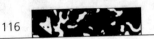
Company) contain his most important commentaries. Robert Warshow's influential essays on popular culture have been collected by Harvard University Press under the title *The Immediate Experience: Movies, Comics, Theatre and other Aspects of Popular Culture* (2001, Harvard University Press). A good source to understanding the debate between Warshow and Dr. Wertham and the history of comics in the United States can be found in Bradford Wright's book *Comic Book Nation: The Transformation of Youth Culture in America* (2001, Johns Hopkins University Press). One final critic of the early 20th century is Dwight MacDonald, who was not as gracious and accepting of popular culture. Paul Gorman has written a helpful intellectual history of MacDonald and early United States cultural criticism, *Left Intellectuals and Popular Culture in Twentieth Century America* (1996, University of North Carolina Press).

The two most important works to consult in regard to Mikhail Bakhtin and popular culture is *The Dialogical Imagination: Four Essays* (Michael Holquist and Caryl Emerson, translators, 1981, University of Texas Press) and *Rabelais and His World* (1984, Indiana University Press). There is also a helpful collection of essays edited by Ken Hirschkop and David Shepard, *Bakhtin and Cultural Theory* (1989, Manchester University Press) that outlines Bakhtin's influence on popular culture and cultural criticism. Marshall McLuhan's best work is *Understanding Media: The Extension of Man* (1964, reissued in 1994, MIT Press). His most famous work, but with fewer details about his ideas, is *The Medium Is the Message: An Inventory of Effects* (1967, Gingko Press).

If you are interested in the debate over the origins of the term "cultural studies," begin with Handel Kashope Wright's essay "Dare We De-centre Birmingham? Troubling the 'Origin' and Trajectories of Cultural Studies" (*European Journal of Cultural Studies* 1:1, pp. 33–56). Wright correctly points out that before the 1970s most of the work we would call cultural studies concentrated on texts and textual analysis. This is true for the U.S., Russian, and Birmingham traditions but, interestingly enough, not the Frankfurt School. To understand how the Birmingham tradition receives credit for beginning cultural studies, see the introduction to the book edited by Henry Jenkins, Tara McPherson, and Jane Shattac, *Hop on Pop* (2003, Duke University Press, pp. 26–42) and Nadine Dolby's introductory essay to a special issue focusing on popular culture in the *Harvard Educational Review*, entitled "Popular Culture and Democratic Practice" (73:3, 2003, pp. 258–284. To understand the perspective of some Birmingham scholars on this issue, see the book dedicated to Stuart Hall's work entitled *Stuart Hall: Critical Dialogues in Cultural Studies* (1996, Routledge) and Angela McRobbie's collection of essays entitled *In the Culture Society: Art, Fashion and Popular Music* (1999, Routledge).

The work of Richard Hoggart and Raymond Williams is instrumental in understanding the rise of the Birmingham School and the break from traditional academic literary scholarship in England. When scholars write about the effect of Hoggart's and Williams' work, it is Williams who garners the most praise. In this author's opinion, Hoggart's *The Uses of Literacy* (1957, republished 1992, Transaction Publishers) is the seminal work in the field. Born into a working-class family, Hoggart tried to stay connected to his roots. This bears proof in his later work, including *Everyday Language and Everyday Life* (2003, Transaction Publishers). Raymond Williams' work is known on a wider scale. His seminal work is *Culture and Society: 1780–1950* (1958, republished 1983, Columbia University Press). Williams also wrote *The Long Revolution* (originally published in 1961, republished 2001, Broadview Press) and *Keywords: A Vocabulary of Culture and Society* (originally published in 1976, republished 1985, Oxford University Press). Anyone interested in his later reflections on his work and society should see his essays in *What I Came to Say* (1989, Hutchinson Radius Press, published posthumously one year after his death).

Stuart Hall's work is immense. Many of his essays that chart his intellectual growth can be found in *Stuart Hall: Critical Dialogues in Cultural Studies* (1996, Routledge),

edited by David Morley and Kuan-Hsing Chen. These essays include his work on ideology, articulation, post-colonialism, race, and the diasporic intellectual. Also worth a look are his book-length commentaries, which are insightful attempts to reconcile leftist theory and the politics of the day. These works include *The Hard Road to Renewal* (1988, Verso Press); *New Times: The Changing Face of Politics in the 1990s* (1989, Lawrence & Wishart Publishers), edited with Martin Jacques; and *Policing the Crisis: 'Mugging,' the State and Law and Order* (1978, MacMillan), edited with Charles Critcher, Tony Jefferson, John Clarke, and Brian Roberts. To understand the depth and impact of Hall's writings, see *Without Guarantees: In Honour of Stuart Hall* (2000, Verso Press), edited by Paul Gilroy, Lawrence Grossberg, and Angela McRobbie. Also, to understand the effect of post-colonialism on cultural studies, read *The Post-Colonial Question: Common Skies, Divided Horizons* (1997, Routledge), edited by Iaim Chambers and Lidia Curti.

The work of Dick Hebdige is an important example of the second generation of scholars from the Birmingham School. His work includes *Subculture: The Meaning of Style* (1989, Routledge), *Cut 'n' Mix: Culture, Identity, and Caribbean Music* (1987, Routledge), and *Hiding in the Light* (1988, Routledge). To understand more about the notion of subculture, one should read the anthology *The Subcultures Reader*, edited by Ken Gelder and Sarah Thornton (1997, Routledge). On Angela McRobbie's work one should read *Postmodernism and Popular Culture* (1994, Routledge), *Feminism and Youth Culture: From Jackie to Just Seventeen* (1991, Routledge), and *In Culture Society: Art, Fashion, and Popular Music* (1999, Routledge). To understand more about the recent push to move cultural studies into the realm of policy formation, see McRobbie's work *British Fashion: Rag Trade or Image Industry* (1998, Routledge) and the work of Tony Bennett, especially *The Birth of the Museum: History, Theory, & Politics* (1995, Routledge).

Paul Gilroy's theories and contributions to cultural studies are found in his trilogy *There Ain't No Black in the*

Union Jack: The Cultural Politics of Race and Nation (1987, Unwin Hyman Press), *Small Acts: Thoughts on the Politics of Black Cultures* (1993, Serpent's Tail), and *The Black Atlantic: Modernity and Double Consciousness* (1993, Harvard University Press). Lawrence Grossberg's work on articulation and the affective can be found in an interview he conducted with Stuart Hall, "On Postmodernism and Articulation," in *Stuart Hall: Critical Dialogues in Cultural Studies* (1996, Routledge, pp. 131–173), *We Gotta Get Out of This Place: Popular Conservatism and Postmodern Culture* (1992, Routledge), and *Dancing in Spite of Myself: Essays on Popular Culture* (1997, Duke University Press).

Anyone interested in the work of James Carey should read his excellent collection of essays in *Communication as Culture: Essays on Media and Society* (1992, Routledge). Carey presents a lucid intellectual history of the connection between the field of communications and cultural studies. He also presents his views in "Reflections on the Project of (American) Cultural Studies," found in *Cultural Studies in Question* (1997, Sage Publications), edited by Marjorie Ferguson and Peter Golding.

Further Readings for Chapter 3

The issue of representation is a fundamental topic of discussion in cultural studies. The best introductory source on representation is *Representation: Cultural Representations and Signifying Practices* (1997, Sage Publications), edited by Stuart Hall. One can pick up almost any book on cultural studies and find a section on representation. Other sources dealing with the mediation of reality include Jean Baudrillard's classic study of reality and its construction, *Simulacra and Simulation* (1994, University of Michigan Press), and Richard Rorty's *Philosophy and the Mirror of Nature* (1981, Princeton University Press). While Baudrillard opened us to the ironies of our simulated realities (e.g., how opinion polls shape opinion), Rorty's work raised questions regarding the representation of nature and truth. Another important work dealing with representation is Donna Haraway's latest work *Modest_witness@*

Second_Millennium.FemaleMan©_Meets_OncoMouse™ (1997, Routledge). In education, McLaren's *Critical Pedagogy and Predatory Culture is an important study on the nature of representation* (1995, Routledge).

The literature on film is as deep as it is fascinating. The classics include André Bazin's two volumes of collected essays, edited by Hugh Gray, *What Is Cinema* (Vol. 1, 1967, and Vol. 2, 1971, University of California Press). Bazin was influential in French cinema studies and theory. His work influenced Giles Deleuze's two-volume work on films: *The Movement-Image,* translated by Hugh Tomlinson and Barbara Habberjam (1986, University Minnesota Press) and *The Time-Image,* translated by Hugh Tomlinson and Robert Galeta (1988, University of Minnesota Press). Deleuze's work is an attempt to adopt Henri Bergson's work on movement and time to cinema. For more on Deleuze's ideas on cinema, see William Reynolds' primer in this series on Deleuze. Another classic is Edwin Panofsky's short essay "Style and Medium in the Motion Pictures." Originally written in 1936, it can be found in the book *Three Essays on Style* (1995, MIT Press), edited by Irving Lavin. In American criticism, Parker Tyler's work, mentioned above, is also important. Those interested in a psychoanalytical approach should also read Siegfred Kracauer's work on German silent films, *From Caligari to Hitler: A Psychological History of German Film* (1947, Princeton University Press). Kracauer gives an excellent history of the German film industry, from its inception to the rise of Adolf Hitler, and he provides detailed studies of many of the early German film classics. Along the lines of Kracauer and the Frankfurt School is Mariam Hansen's book *Babel & Babylon: Spectatorship in American Silent Film* (1991, Harvard University Press). To understand the full technological history of film, Lev Manovich's work, mentioned in Further Readings for Chapter 1, is essential. Stanley Cavell is still probably the most cited American critic of film. A philosopher by training, Cavell brought his philosophical training to all his works on film. His most famous work is *The World Viewed: Reflections on the Ontology of Film* (1971, Viking Press).

However, if you are interested in his views, also read *Pursuits of Happiness: Hollywood Comedy of Remarriage* (1984, Harvard University Press) and his introductory essay to Robert Warshow's collection of essays *Immediate Experience* (2001, Harvard University Press).

The work on television is not as extensive as that on film, an issue discussed in Chapter 5. However, the literature that does exist is monumental. Marshall McLuhan's views on television can be found in his book *Understanding Media: The Extensions of Man* (1964/ 1994, MIT Press). Perhaps the most important philosophical essay on television is Samuel Weber's essay "Television: Set and Screen," found in a book of his essays entitled *Mass Mediauras: Form, Technics, Media* (1996, Stanford University Press). Raymond Williams' views can be found in his book *Television: Technology and Cultural Form* (1974/ 1992, Wesleyan University Press). The reprint issue contains an introductory essay by Lynn Spigel, the premier television historian in the United States. Anyone interested in Spigel's work should consult *Make Room for TV: Television and the Family Ideal in Postwar* America (1992, University of Chicago Press) and the book *Telvision and Cultural Studies* (1999, Routledge), which she edited. Jacques Derrida's perspectives on television are collected in a series of interviews with Bernard Steigler, *Echographies of Television* (2002, Polity). Derrida is the most important European philosopher of the last 40 years and these essays demonstrate his depth and commitment to democratic ideals. They also show his sense of humor. When he was asked what type of television he likes to watch, he replied, "All kinds of things, the best and the worst. Sometimes I watch bad soap operas, French or American" (2002, p. 138). Bernard Steigler is worth mentioning because he is just beginning to be translated into English and is offering a new look at the effect of technology and technocultures on the world. Douglas Kellner is one of the most prolific writers on popular culture and television. His first study was *Television and the Crisis of Democracy* (1990, Westview Press). His ideas are also best expressed in *Media Culture* (1995, Routledge).

John Fiske's work is essential for understanding popular culture and is also discussed in the section on fan cultures. In regard to television, Fiske's major works are *Television Culture* (1987, Routledge) and *Reading the Popular* (1989, Unwin Hyman Publishers). In both of these books, he offers a semiotic reading of popular culture. Other sources that offer a textual approach to television is the collection *Remote Control: Television, Audiences & Cultural Power* (1991, Routledge), edited by Ellen Seiter, Hans Borchers, Gabrielle Kreutzner, and Eva-Maria Warth; and Lynn Joyrich's study of gender and television, *Reviewing Reception: Television, Gender, and Postmodern Culture* (1996, Indiana University Press).

The literature on *Roseanne* is intriguing because of the material. The most important essay on *Roseanne* is Julie Bettie's work, "Class Dismissed?: *Roseanne* and the Changing Face of Working-Class Iconography" (*Social Text* 14:4, 1995, pp. 125–149). Another interesting essay on *Roseanne* is Janet Lee's "Subversive Sitcoms: Roseanne as Inspiration for Feminist Resistance" (*Women's Studies* 21, 1992, pp. 87–101). To this author's knowledge, there are no detailed studies that focus on *The Waltons*. (But this author, like many fans, wholeheartedly endorses it and believes that the show is one of the best ever created for television. The scripts are well written, the acting award-winning, and the progressive messages timeless.)

The scholarship on music is immense. The source for understanding the depth and passion Adorno has for musical criticism is the collection edited by Richard Leppert, *Essays on Music* (2002, University of California Press). On the history of rock-and-roll music, Greil Marcus' work is essential. *Lipstick Traces: A Secret History of the Twentieth Century* (1990, Harvard University Press) and *Mystery Train: Images of America in Rock 'n' Roll Music* (1997, Plume Publishers) are good places to start. Simon Firth and Andrew Goodwin's anthology *On Record: Rock, Pop, and the Written Word* (2000, Routledge), with its numerous critical essays on rock, is also a helpful source for understanding its history. Another useful source is Angela McRobbie's review essays included in her book *In the*

Culture Society: Art, Fashion, and Popular Music (1999, Routledge). One of the best studies of gender and music is Robin Roberts' *Ladies First: Women in Videos* (1996, University of Mississippi Press). Roberts demonstrates that from rock, country, folk, and hip-hop women have found creative outlets in music to express important issues such as spousal violence and economic independence. If you are interested in iteration as a concept, see J. Hillis Miller's *Speech Acts in Literature* (2001, Stanford University Press).

The scholarship on hip-hop grows almost as fast as the industry. If you are interested in hip-hop within the context of African American history and music, the two places to start are Mark Anthony Neal's *What the Music Said: Black Popular Music and Black Public Culture* (1999, Routledge) and Craig Werner's *A Change Is Gonna Come: Music, Race & the Soul of America* (1998, Plume Publishers). The main historical source of the development of hip-hop is Tricia Rose's *Black Noise: Rap Music and Black Culture in Contemporary America* (1994, University Press of New England). The commentary on the style, rhythm, and bravado of hip-hop is long. Andrew Ross and Tricia Rose's collection *Microphone Fiends: Youth Music & Youth Culture* (1994, Routledge) is a good place to start, so is *Droppin' Science: Critical Essays on Rap Music and Hip Hop Culture* (1996, Temple University Press), edited by William Eric Perkins. Other sources are Imani Perry's essay "'I Am Still Thirsty': A Theorization on the Authority and Cultural Location of Afrocentrism," which can be found in *Freedom's Plow* (1993, Routledge), edited by Theresa Perry and James Fraser. Also noteworthy are bell hooks' selected essays on hip-hop found in *Outlaw Culture: Resisting Representations* (1994, Routledge) and Russell Potter's book *Spectacular Vernaculars: Hip Hop and the Politics of Postmodernism* (1995, SUNY Press). A source for understanding the global impact of hip-hop is *Global Noise: Rap and Hip Hop outside the USA* (2001, Wesleyan University Press), edited by Tony Mitchell.

The work on fan cultures is intriguing. To understand the early development of spectatorship, see Mariam

Hansen's work *Babel & Babylon: Spectatorship in American Silent Film* (1991, Harvard University Press) and *Cinema and Invention of Modern Life* (1995, University of California Press), edited by Leo Charney and Vanessa Schwartz, which includes an essay by Hansen. On fan cultures, Henry Jenkins' work is essential: *Textual Poachers: Television Fans & Partiipatory Culture* (1992, Routledge). Also see Constance Penley's important book, *NASA/Trek* (1997, Verso), which chronicles the historical relationship between fan cultures, science fiction, and space travel. To understand Michel de Certeau's idea of textual poaching, see his work *The Practice of Everyday Life* (1988, University of California Press). John Fiske's book *Power Plays Power Works* is an important theoretical piece that demonstrates the effect that cultural studies theories can have on social justice and political action. Daniel Cavicchi's work, *Tramps like Us: Music and Meaning among Springsteen Fans* (1998, Oxford University Press) is an excellent example of the contributions ethnographers have made to our understanding of culture. If you are interested in Cavicchi's ideas, also read Toby Daspit's interview with Cavicchi in the *Journal of Curriculum Theorizing* (18:2, 1992, pp. 89–98).

Further Readings for Chapter 4

On the cultural studies of science, the literature is as grand as it is detailed. Thomas Kuhn's landmark book *The Structure of Scientific Revolutions* (1962, University of Chicago Press) is the essential starting point for anyone interested in science studies. His subsequent ideas can be studied in *Essential Tension* (1979, University of Chicago Press), a collection of his essays that came out after *The Structure* appeared. Also, his essay "Reflections on My Critics" in the book edited by I. Lakatos and A. Musgrave, *Criticism and Growth of Knowledge* (1970, Cambridge University Press) is important and insightful. The most interesting commentary on Kuhn's work is Steve Fuller's essay in *History and Theory*, entitled "Being There with Thomas Kuhn: A Parable for Postmodern Times" (31:3, 1992, pp. 241–275). Paul Feyerabend's book *Against Method* (1975, Verso Press) is also an important source to understand the culture of science. The work of Katherine Hayles is important as well. Her first work sets the stage for her other endeavors, *The Cosmic Web: Scientific Field Models & Literary Strategies in the 20th Century* (1984, Cornell University Press), followed by *Chaos Bound: Orderly Disorder in Contemporary Literature and Science* (1990, Cornell University Press) and *How We Became Posthuman: Virtual Bodies in Cybernetics, Literature, and Informatics* (1999, University of Chicago Press). Anyone interested in her second book should find the volume she edited, *Chaos and Order: Complex Dynamics in Literature and Science* (1991, University of Chicago Press), just as illuminating. The work of Peter Galison is monumental. His most influential book is *Image and Logic: A Material Culture of Microphysics* (1997, University of Chicago Press). Other important works from Galison include *How Experiments End* (1987, University of Chicago Press), *Big Science: The Growth of Large-Scale Research* (1992, Stanford University Press), and the book he edited with David Stump, *The Disunity of Science: Boundaries, Contexts, and Power* (1996, Stanford University Press). Timothy Lenoir's ideas are explained in his book *Instituting Science: The Cultural Production of Scientific Disciplines* (1997, Stanford University Press). If anyone is interested in his current work, see the 2003 special issue of the journal *Configurations* (10:2).

Actor network theory is dominated by French scholars. Bruno Latour is the most notable scholar in this area. His most cited work is *Science in Action: How to Follow Scientists and Engineers through Society* (1987, Harvard University Press). His work with Steve Woolgar, *Laboratory Life: The Construction of Scientific Facts* (1986, Princeton University Press), is also an important guide to actor network theory. Latour has contributed other important works as well, including *The Pasteurization of France* (1988, Harvard University Press) and his most recent work *Pandora's Hope: Essays on the Reality of Science Studies* (1999, Harvard University Press). The work of Michel Callon is also essential for understanding actor network theory. See his chapter entitled "Struggles and Negotiations to

Decide What is Problematic and What is Not: The Sociologics of Translation," in *The Social Process of Scientific Investigation* (1981, Reidel Press, pp. 197–220), edited by Karin Knorr, Roger Krohn, and Richard Whitley; and the book he co-edited with John Law and Arie Rip, *Mapping the Dynamics of Science and Technology* (1986, MacMillan Press). Harry Collins and Martin Kusch have written an important introduction to actor network theory entitled *The Shape of Actions: What Humans and Machines Can Do* (1998, MIT Press). It is a wonderful look at the many ways in which humans and machines interact to construct an understanding of nature. An interesting ethnographic example of actor network theory is Karin Knorr Cetina's work *Epistemic Cultures: How the Sciences Make Knowledge* (1999, Harvard University Press). Knorr Cetina looks at the science of particle physics and the smaller but just as important endeavors of molecular biology research.

Within all of these traditions, there are numerous examples of scholars who do traditional anthropological, historical, and philosophical work. The best example of the anthropology of science is Sharon Traweek's study *Beamtimes and Lifetimes: The World of High Energy Physicists* (1988, Harvard University Press). Traweek has spent the good part of 30 years studying the interactions of Japanese and American physicists. Another example of the anthropology of science is the work of Paul Rabinow, who is well known for becoming a part of the research process and acting as a consultant to science projects that help scientists and science administrators understand their cultures. His most recent work centers on genetics and biotechnology and includes *French DNA: Trouble in Purgatory* (1999, University of Chicago Press) and *Making PCR: A Story of Biotechnology* (1996, University of Chicago Press). The most interesting works in the history of science is the book by Steven Shapin and Simon Schaffer, *Leviathan and the Air-Pump: Hobbes, Boyle, and the Experimental Life* (1985, Princeton University Press) and by Shapin, *A Social History of Truth: Civility and Science in Seventeenth-Century England* (1994, University of Chicago Press). In both of these cases, Shapin and Schaffer demonstrate how truth and laboratory cultures are shaped by historical events, debates between rivals, social class, and often pettiness. Besides Kuhn and Feyerabend's work, there are other interesting works in the philosophy of science. Babette Babich's *Nietzsche's Philosophy of Science: Reflecting Science on the Ground of Art and Life* (1994, SUNY Press) is a good example of how Nietzsche's idea of perspectivism is applicable to science. Another important philosopher of science is Arkady Plotnitsky, especially his *Complimentarity: Anti-Epistemology after Bohr and Derrida* (1994, Duke University Press), which demonstrates the similarities between the work of Bohr and Heisenberg in science and the philosophy of Derrida, and *The Knowable and the Unknowable: Modern Science, Nonclassical Thought, and the 'Two Cultures,'* which is his contribution to the debates surrounding the so-called "science wars."

The literature dealing with the materiality of culture and the role of literature in the cultural studies of science is immense. One should begin with the theoretical writings of J. Hillis Miller, found in one of his more recent books, *Black Holes* (1999, Stanford University Press). Also please refer to Kittler's work cited in Chapter 1. George Landow has done groundbreaking work that merges literature with technology. His ideas are best represented in his book *Hypertext 2.0: The Convergence of Contemporary Critical Theory and Technology* (1992, Johns Hopkins University Press). The book *Reading Matters: Narratives in the New Media Ecology* (1997, Cornell University Press), edited by Joseph Tabbi and Michael Wutz, contains essays commenting on the merging of media technology and literature. So does the book *Materialities of Communication* (1994, Stanford University Press), edited by Hans Ulrich Gumbrecht and K. Ludwig Pfeiffer. William Paulson's monograph *Literary Culture in a World Transformed* (2001, Cornell University Press) is an excellent source for understanding the two cultures and interdisciplinary work in the university. Two important theoretical treatises on the merging of literary studies with information technology are

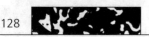

R.L. Rutsky's *High Techne: Art and Technology from the Machine Aesthetic to the Posthuman* (1999, University of Minnesota Press) and Mark Hansen's *Embodying Technesis: Technology beyond Writing* (2000, University of Michigan Press). Anyone interested in Rutsky's ideas should see this author's interview with him in the special issue of the *Journal of Curriculum Theorizing* (summer 2002, 18:2, pp. 7–18), entitled "It's a Posthuman World."

The literature on technocultures is equally impressive. On the history of the future of the posthuman condition, start with N. Katherine Hayles' *How We Became Posthuman: Virtual Bodies in Cybernetics, Literature, and Informatics* (1999, University of Chicago). Donna Haraway's work is also important, including her latest book, mentioned in the Further Readings for Chapter 3. Her most famous essay is her 1985 article "A Cyborg Manifesto: Science, Technology, and Socialist Feminism in the Late Twentieth Century" the journal *Socialist Review* (80, 1985, pp. 65–108). *Simians, Cyborgs, and Women: The Reinvention of Nature* (1991, Routledge) contains a reprint of "The Cyborg Manifesto," plus other illuminating chapters dealing with Haraway's ideas on technoscience. Chris Hables Gray, a Haraway student, has an excellent introductory book on the posthuman condition called *Cyborg Citizen* (2001, Routledge), and his book *The Cyborg Handbook* (1995, Routledge), which he edited with Steven Mentor and Heidi Figueroa-Sarriera, is an important guide to understanding the posthuman.

In regard to technocultures, the literature seems limitless. For a theoretical account of technocultures, undergraduates should begin with Jay Bolter and Richard Grusin's *Remediation: Understanding New Media* (2000, MIT). It is a freshmen literature textbook that does not "dumb down" the issues for undergraduates. Lev Manovich's work mentioned in Chapter 3 is also essential, as is Pierre Levy's theoretical look at virtual realities, *Becoming Virtual: Reality in the Digital Age* (1998, Plenum Trade Publishers).

The accounts of technocultures in action are interesting. One should start with either Allecquère Stone's *The War of Desire and Technology at the Close of the Mechanical Age* (1998, MIT) or Sherry Turkle's *Life on the Screen: Identity in the Age of the Internet* (1995, Touchstone Publishers). There are numerous interesting collections of essays, including *Internet Culture* (1997, Routledge), edited by David Porter; the collection *Cyberspace, Cyberbodies, Cuberpunk: Cultures of Technological Embodiment* (1995, Sage Publishers), edited by Mike Featherstone and Roger Burrows; *Technoculture* (1991, University of Minnesota Press), edited by Andrew Ross and Constance Penley; Timothy Druckery's collection *Electronic Culture: Technology and Visual Representation* (1996, Apperture Books); a collection by Beth Kolko, Lisa Nakamura, and Gilbert Rodman entitled *Race on Cyberspace* (2000, Routledge); and the collection by Gabriel Brahm Jr. and Mark Driscoll *Prosthetic Territories: Politics and Hypertechnologies* (1995, Westview Press). There are single-author books of interest as well, including Pierre Lévy's latest book *CyberCulture* (2001, University of Minnesota Press); Anna Balsamo's focus on technology and gender in *Technology of the Gendered Body: Reading Cyborg Women* (1997, Duke University Press) and Kevin Robins' and Frank Webster's *Times of the Technoculture: From the Information Society to the Virtual Life* (1999, Routledge).

There are numerous places to start in order to understand the science debates. Alan Sokal's article "A Physicist Experiments with Cultural Studies," which exposed his journal submission hoax, appeared in the journal that specializes in academic gossip, *Lingua Franca* (May/June, 1996, pp. 62–64). Another source to consult is Gerald Holton's *Science and Anti-Science* (1994, Harvard University Press). The best book to capture the position of critics of the science studies movement is *A House Built on Sand: Exposing Postmodernist Myths about Science* (1998, Oxford University Press), edited by Noretta Koertga, which includes Philip Kitcher's article "A Plea for Science Studies" (pp. 32–56). Although the best produced by critics, the articles in this book still are pleas to return to the

"good ole days" when scientists were kings and other academics knew their inferior stations in the ordained hierarchy of knowledge. By far the two worst rants in the science debates are Alan Sokal's and Jean Bricmont's book *Fashionable Nonsense: Postmodern Intellectuals' Abuse of Science* (1998, Picador USA) and Paul Gross' and Norm Levitt's *Higher Superstition: The Academic Left and Its Quarrels with Science* (1994, Johns Hopkins University Press). Rebuttals can be found in *Science Wars*, which is edited by Andrew Ross and which includes Sharon Traweek's essay on thinking in more than one way about science (1996, Duke University Press). There are also Ian Hacking's book *The Social Construction of What?* (1999, Harvard University Press) and Arkady Plotnitsky's book the *Knowable and Unknowable*. Anyone interested in the politics of academic work can read this author's contribution to the debate in *Rethinking Academic Politics in (Re)Unified Germany and the United States* (1999, Routledge/Falmer Press).

Further Readings for Chapter 5

The interview between Lawrence Grossberg and Handel Wright can be found in *Review of Education/Pedagogy/Cultural Studies* (2000, pp. 1–25) and is titled "Pressing, Promising, and Paradoxical: Larry Grossberg on Education and Cultural Studies." On key early texts defining the meaning of the cultural studies of education is Paul Willis' *Learning to Labor: How Working Class Kids Get Working Class Jobs* (Columbia University Press, 1977). To honor the impact of this work and mark the 25th year since its publication, Nadine Dolby and Greg Dimitriadis have edited a collection of essays entitled *Learning to Labor in New Times* (2004, Routledge). Included in this collection is an interview with Paul Willis that includes an intellectual biography of his development and education. Leslie Roman and Linda Christian-Smith's work *Becoming Feminine: The Politics of Popular Culture* (1988, Falmer Press) marks the beginning point of the serious consideration of the relationships among gender formations, popular culture, and the schooling processes.

Henry Giroux's work represents the most detailed attempt to connect popular culture and schooling to democracy. His first attempt at doing cultural studies was a book he edited with Roger Simon entitled *Popular Culture: Schooling and Everyday Life* (Bergin & Garvey, 1989). His most recent works include *Living Dangerously: Multiculturalism and the Politics of Difference* (1993, Peter Lang Publishing), *Disturbing Pleasures: Learning Popular Culture* (1994, Routledge), *Fugitive Cultures: Race, Violence, & Youth* (1996, Routledge), *Channel Surfing: Race, Talk, and the Destruction of Today's Youth* (1999, St. Martin's Press), *The Mouse That Roared: Disney and the End of Innocence* (1999, Rowman & Littlefield), *Stealing Innocence: Youth, Corporate Power, and the Politics of Culture* (2000, St. Martin's Press), and *Breaking into Movies: Film and the Culture of Politics* (2002, Blackwell Publishers).

The literature on childhood studies is growing every year and represents one of the most vibrant fields of study in education. There are numerous books that provide excellent insights into this new field, including the already-mentioned *Kinderculture: The Corporate Construction of Childhood*, edited by Shirley Steinberg and Joe Kincheloe (1997, Westview Publishers); and *Kidworld: Childhood Studies, Global Perspectives, and Education* (2002, Peter Lang Publishing) by Gaile Cannella and Joe Kincheloe. Other important works in the field include Bernadette Baker's study *In Perpetual Motion: Theories of Power, Educational History, and the Child* (2001, Peter Lang Publishing) and Lisa Goldstein's *Teaching with Love: A Feminist Approach to Early Childhood Education* (1997, Peter Lang Publishing) and *Reclaiming Caring in Teaching and Teacher Education* (2002, Peter Lang Publishing). Henry Jenkins edited an excellent anthology on children's culture, *The Children's Culture Reader* (1998, New York University Press). Radhika Viruru has tried to extend childhood studies into the realm of post-colonial studies with her work *Early Childhood Education: Postcolonial Perspectives from India* (2001, Sage Publications). Anyone interested in the latest scholarship

in childhood studies should read Viruru and Cannella's section, "Childhood and Cultural Studies," in the *Journal of Curriculum Theorizing*.

The literature on consumption, corporate culture, and education is just as impressive. Jane Kenway and Elizabeth Bullen's *Consuming Children: Education-Entertainment-Advertising* (2001, Open University Press) is important, as is Alex Molnar's study *Giving Kids the Business: The Commercialization of America's Schools* (1996, Westview Press). Also of note is Peter McLaren's work *Critical Pedagogy and Predatory Culture* (1995, Routledge). One of the few studies conducted by an educational psychologist that tries to understand the effect of popular culture and gender identity is Valerie Walkerdine's *Daddy's Girl: Young Girls and Popular Culture* (1997, Harvard University Press). Another important work in the field of education is Joe Kincheloe's *The Sign of the Burger: McDonald's and the Culture of Power* (2002, Temple University Press).

The work on critical media literacy continues to grow. The influential book by Peter McLaren, Rhonda Hammer, David Shole, and Susan Reilly entitled *Rethinking Media Literacy: A Critical Pedagogy of Representation* (1995, Peter Lang Publishing) represents the first major attempt to connect media studies with critical pedagogy. Ladislaus Semali has continued this tradition in his book *Literacy in Multimedia America* (2001, Routledge). Brian Goldfarb's *Visual Pedagogy: Media Studies in and beyond the Classroom* (2002, Duke University Press) represents a slight break from critical media literacy in that Goldfarb suggests the word literacy still equates and compares the visual with the written word.

In the area of history and films, Robert Rosenstone's work is essential. They include *Revisioning the Past: Film and the Construction of a New Past* (1995, Princeton University Press) and *Visions of the Past: The Challenge of Film to Our Idea of History* (1995, Harvard University Press). Vivian Sobchack has edited an interesting collection on the topic of film and representation entitled *The Persistance of History: Cinema, Television, and the Modern*

Event (1996, Routledge). Peter Seixas' work dealing with how students interpret the past through film is important and can be found in *Theory and Research in Social Education* (1994, pp. 281–304), entitled "Students' Understanding of Historical Significance." Those readers interested in the idea of popular culture as a form of critical pedagogy should see *Popular Culture and Critical Pedagogy: Reading, Constructing, Connecting* (2000, Garland Publishing), edited by Toby Daspit and John A. Weaver; and Houston Baker's work *Black Studies, Rap, and the Academy* (1993, University of Chicago Press).

The work of cultural curriculum studies is a young but growing field within education. To understand the development of William Reynolds' ideas and shift to popular culture, see his work *Curriculum: A River Runs through It* (2003, Peter Lang Publishing). Susan Edgerton's work can be found in *Translating the Curriculum: Multiculturalism into Cultural Studies* (1996, Routledge). Peter Appelbaum's major work in the area of popular culture is found in *Popular Culture, Educational Discourse, and Mathematics* (1995, SUNY Press); in the chapter "Cyborg Selves: Saturday Morning Magic and Magical Morality" in *Potent Fictions: Children's Literacy and the Challenge of Popular Culture* (1996, Routledge), edited by Toby Daspit and John A. Weaver; and in *Popular Culture and Critical Pedagogy* (2000, Garland Publishing, pp. 83–115).

The importance of science fiction in teaching can be found in Noel Gough's groundbreaking work *Laboratories in Fiction: Science Education and Popular Media* (1993, Deakin University Press) and in *Science Fiction Curriculum, Cyborg Teachers, and Youth Cultures* edited by John A. Weaver, Karen Anijar, and Toby Daspit (2004, Peter Lang Publishing, pp. 89–108). Anyone interested in the scholarly literature on science fiction should consult Marleen Barr's *Lost in Space: Probing Feminist Science Fiction and Beyond* (1993, University of North Carolina Press), Robin Roberts' *A New Species: Gender and Science in Science Fiction* (1993, University of Illinois Press), and

Vivian Sobchak's *Screening Space: The American Science Fiction Film* (1987, Ungar Publishers).

Anyone interested in the general question concerning popular culture and education should consult three important books: *Small Screens: Television for Children* (2002, Leicester University Press), edited by David Buckingham, which provides non-American perspectives on popular culture; Eugene Provenzo's study *Video Kids: Making Sense of Nintendo* (1991, Harvard University Press); and *Potent Fictions: Children's Literacy and the Challenge of Popular Culture* (1996, Routledge), edited by Mary Hilton.

The work of Greg Dimitriadis is represented in *Performing Identity/Performing Culture: Hip Hop as Text, Pedagogy, and Lived Practice* (2001, Peter Lang Publishing); *Friendships, Cliques, and Gangs: Young Black Men Coming of Age in Urban America* (2003, Teacher's College Press); and his co-authored text with Cameron McCarthy, *Reading and Teaching the Postcolonial: From Baldwin to Basquiat and Beyond* (2001, Teacher's College Press). Anyone interested in Cameron McCarthy's ideas concerning popular culture can read his book (co-edited with Warren Crichlow) *Race, Identity, and Representation in Education* (1993, Routledge).

Index

Peter Lang PRIMERS
in Education

Peter Lang Primers are designed to provide a brief and concise introduction or supplement to specific topics in education. Although sophisticated in content, these primers are written in an accessible style, making them perfect for undergraduate and graduate classroom use. Each volume includes a glossary of key terms and a References and Resources section.

Other published and forthcoming volumes cover such topics as:

- Standards
- Popular Culture
- Critical Pedagogy
- Literacy
- Higher Education
- John Dewey
- Feminist Theory and Education
- Studying Urban Youth Culture
- Multiculturalism through Postformalism
- Creative Problem Solving
- Teaching the Holocaust
- Piaget and Education
- Deleuze and Education
- Foucault and Education

Look for more Peter Lang Primers to be published soon. To order other volumes, please contact our Customer Service Department:

> 800-770-LANG (within the US)
> 212-647-7706 (outside the US)
> 212-647-7707 (fax)

To find out more about this and other Peter Lang book series, or to browse a full list of education titles, please visit our website:

www.peterlangusa.com